Teaching Other Subjects through English

Titles in the Resource Books for Teachers series

Beginners
Peter Grundy

Classroom Dynamics
Jill Hadfield

Conversation
Rob Nolasco and Lois Arthur

Creative Poetry Writing
Jane Spiro

Cultural Awareness
Barry Tomalin and Susan Stempleski

Dictionaries
Jon Wright

Drama
Charlyn Wessels

English for Specific Purposes
Keith Harding

Exam Classes
Peter May

Film
Susan Stempleski and Barry Tomalin

Global Issues
Ricardo Sampedro and Susan Hillyard

Grammar
Scott Thornbury

Grammar Dictation
Ruth Wajnryb

Homework
Lesley Painter

The Internet
Scott Windeatt, David Hardisty,
and D. Eastment

Learner-based Teaching
Colin Campbell and Hanna Kryszewska

Letters
Nicky Burbidge, Peta Gray, Sheila Levy,
and Mario Rinvolucri

Listening
Goodith White

Literature
Alan Duff and Alan Maley

Music and Song
Tim Murphey

Newspapers
Peter Grundy

Project Work 2nd edition
Diana L. Fried-Booth

Pronunciation
Clement Laroy

Role Play
Gillian Porter Ladousse

Storybuilding
Jane Spiro

Teenagers
Gordon Lewis

Vocabulary 2nd edition
John Morgan and Mario Rinvolucri

Writing 2nd edition
Tricia Hedge

Primary Resource Books

Art and Crafts with Children
Andrew Wright

Assessing Young Learners
Sophie Ioannou-Georgiou
and Pavlos Pavlou

Creating Chants and Songs
Carolyn Graham

Creating Stories with Children
Andrew Wright

Drama with Children
Sarah Phillips

Games for Children
Gordon Lewis with Günther Bedson

The Internet and Young Learners
Gordon Lewis

Projects with Young Learners
Diane Phillips, Sarah Burwood,
and Helen Dunford

Storytelling with Children
Andrew Wright

Very Young Learners
Vanessa Reilly and Sheila M. Ward

Writing with Children
Jackie Reilly and Vanessa Reilly

Young Learners
Sarah Phillips

Resource Books for Teachers

series editor Alan Maley

Teaching Other Subjects Through English

Sheelagh Deller
Christine Price

OXFORD
UNIVERSITY PRESS

OXFORD
UNIVERSITY PRESS

Great Clarendon Street, Oxford OX2 6DP

Oxford University Press is a department of the University of Oxford.
It furthers the University's objective of excellence in research, scholarship,
and education by publishing worldwide in

Oxford New York

Auckland Cape Town Dar es Salaam Hong Kong Karachi
Kuala Lumpur Madrid Melbourne Mexico City Nairobi
New Delhi Shanghai Taipei Toronto

With offices in

Argentina Austria Brazil Chile Czech Republic France Greece
Guatemala Hungary Italy Japan Poland Portugal Singapore
South Korea Switzerland Thailand Turkey Ukraine Vietnam

OXFORD and OXFORD ENGLISH are registered trade marks of
Oxford University Press in the UK and in certain other countries

Photocopying

ISBN-13: 987 019 442578 0

Printed in China

Acknowledgements

The many teachers of many subjects we have worked with on different courses. They have been the inspiration and the reason for this book.

Julia Sallabank for her guidance and perseverance.

Katie Plumb and Simon Marshall for their pertinent and valuable support and contribution.

Richard and Sarah for their encouragement and patience.

Mario Rinvolucri who has always given us his whole-hearted and generous support.

The authors and publisher are grateful to those who have given permission to reproduce the following extracts and adaptations of copyright material:

Visnja Anic for permission to adapt an activity from *Way To Go – Teacher's Book* (Skolska Knjiga, Zagreb, 2001).

Paul Davies for permission to adapt 'Guess My Word'.

Keith Kelly for permission to adapt 'Skill areas for CLIL'.

Christine Frank and Mario Rinvolucri for permission to reproduce 'One question—many answers' from *Grammar in Action* (Pergamon, 1983).

Mario Rinvolucri for permission to reproduce 'Oral sentence expansion' from *Humanising Your Coursebook* (English Teaching Professional/Delta, 2002).

www.design-technology.org (1.2).

Letts GCSE Success Guide: Business Studies © David Frost, 2001 (1.3).

'How Food Preparation Works' by Marshall Brain from http://home.howstuffworks.com/food-preservation (1.6).

Reeko's Mad Scientist Lab www.spartechsoftware.com/reeko (1.10).

Sources of other information or adapted material:

www.digitalbritain.com (Introduction).

Pair Work 2 by Peter Watcyn Jones (Penguin, 1997) (3.5).

Although every effort has been made to trace and contact copyright holders before publication, this has not been possible in some cases. We apologize for any apparent infringement of copyright and if notified, the publisher will be pleased to rectify any errors or omissions at the earliest opportunity.

We would like to thank the following for permission to reproduce photographs and illustrative material:

Hardlines, Charlbury, Oxon/OUP (p. 53)
Bridgeman Art Library (English School/Private collection) (p. 119)
Food Features (p. 27)
HarperCollins (p. 116)
Granada Medai (p. 131–2).

Contents

2 Teaching and activating key vocabulary

Contents | **xi**

Activity	Demo subject	Aims	

7 Project work

The authors and series editor

Sheelagh Deller is an experienced teacher, teacher trainer, trainer trainer, and ELT author. She has worked primarily for Pilgrims and the British Council. She has long experience in training trainers and teachers from all over the world, and is a regular plenary speaker at international conferences. Over the last four years she has run two-week courses at Pilgrims for teachers of other subjects in English (CLIL), and has drawn on this experience to develop this methodology. She has written a number of ELT books, which include a coursebook, some workbooks, teachers' books, teachers' resource books, and a book of photocopiable materials. Her latest book, *Using the Mother Tongue,* with Mario Rinvolucri, was published by Delta in 2002.

Christine Price is a state qualified teacher with many years of experience in primary and secondary schools in the UK. She has taught English language and literature, history, physical education, biology, commercial subjects, dance and drama at Secondary level, and all subjects across the curriculum at primary level. Over the last twelve years she has worked for Pilgrims as a teacher trainer and business trainer. She runs courses for Pilgrims in the UK and abroad, in Business English, British Studies, secondary and primary language, and methodology. She draws on her experience in the 'real' classroom situation for a practical, hands-on approach to teacher training.

Alan Maley worked for the British Council from 1962 to 1988, serving as English Language Officer in Yugoslavia, Ghana, Italy, France, and China, and as Regional Representative in South India (Madras). From 1988 to 1993 he was Director-General of the Bell Educational Trust, Cambridge. From 1993 to 1998 he was Senior Fellow in the Department of English Language and Literature of the National University of Singapore, and from 1998 to 2002 he was Director of the graduate programme at Assumption University, Bangkok. He is currently a freelance consultant. Among his publications are *Literature*, in this series, *Beyond Words*, *Sounds Interesting*, *Sounds Intriguing*, *Words*, *Variations on a Theme*, and *Drama Techniques in Language Learning* (all with Alan Duff), *The Mind's Eye* (with Françoise Grellet and Alan Duff), *Learning to Listen* and *Poem into Poem* (with Sandra Moulding), *Short and Sweet*, and *The English Teacher's Voice*.

Foreword

Content and Language Integrated Learning (CLIL) has attracted great interest in recent years, especially in Europe but increasingly more widely in the world. This is undoubtedly linked to the expansion of subject teaching in English, whether in state pilot experimental schools, universities, or international schools. This in its turn rides on the back of the tendency for parents to want their children to make an earlier start in learning English. Many children are now relatively proficient in general English by the time they reach secondary school age and need something more than a re-hash of what they have already learnt. These trends go hand in hand with the perception of English as the international language of choice for career development, and show no sign of slackening.

The belief underlying CLIL is that teaching subjects through English provides a better preparation for professional life than teaching English as a subject empty of content. There are, too, clear motivational advantages in teaching English for a well-defined purpose which is perceived as relevant by the students.

CLIL has recently become something of a cult movement, and there are many articles and even some books which discuss its theoretical foundations. There is, however, a relative dearth of books offering practical, classroom-tested ideas on ways to implement a CLIL approach. This book aims to go some way towards meeting the need for such a practical resource.

Teachers of CLIL are of two main kinds: subject teachers who find they need to teach their subject in English—with all the attendant difficulties of limited proficiency in English, and limited familiarity with language teaching methodology—and language teachers who are assigned to teach subject matter in English—with problems of unfamiliarity with subject areas. This book will be of special help to the former, but also offers ideas to help the latter.

Each activity focuses on a particular subject area—mathematics, physics, history, etc.—and shows in detail how it could be applied to teach an aspect of that subject. However, for each activity, there are a number of suggestions on how to apply the activity to other subject areas. In line with the philosophy of this series therefore, teachers are therefore encouraged to pick up the ideas but to adapt them to suit their own specific circumstances.

Given the huge expansion in the provision of subject teaching through English, the relative lack of preparation of some teachers confronted by the need to carry this out, and the shortage of well-tried materials for doing it, this book will prove to be a very welcome resource.

Alan Maley

Introduction

Who is this book for?

- Subject teachers who teach their subject through English to students aged 11–18.
- Subject teachers who teach their subject through other target languages.
- English language teachers who use other subjects to teach English to students aged 11–18.
- Subject teachers who have multi-lingual classes.
- Teachers who support students aged 11–18 across the curriculum in English.
- Subject teachers who want to widen their repertoire of classroom activities.
- Pre-service and in-service teacher trainers who train teachers to teach subject matter through a foreign language.
- Trainee teachers and those on in-service teacher development courses.

Background: Content and Language Integrated Learning

The last five years have seen a massive expansion of Content and Language Integrated Learning (CLIL). CLIL is now becoming common practice throughout many countries in Europe, Asia, Africa, South America and the Far East. To get a better understanding of the place of CLIL it is helpful to compare different types of foreign language teaching.

1 Foreign language teaching for general purposes

This is language-led and applies the language to different situations and topics in order to illustrate the language points. It uses language teaching methodology and the assessment is based on language level.

2 Foreign language teaching for work purposes (ESP)

This is also language-led, but the content is determined and influenced by the work purpose. It uses language teaching methodology and the assessment is based on language level.

3 Cross-curricular foreign language teaching

This is language teaching using content from across the curricula. It is taught by language teachers who use cross-curricular content, and is assessed on language level.

4 CLIL—Subject teaching through a foreign language

This is entirely subject-led and the subject dictates what language support is needed. The language is one part of the process, rather than an end in itself. It is assessed on subject knowledge. (See 'CLIL methodology' below.) It may be taught by a subject teacher, or a foreign language teacher. In some cases it is taught by both teachers, which is an ideal scenario, though as this is a resource-heavy option it is less common.

There is a fundamental difference in the use of language between the language class and the content class. In the language class the four skills (reading, listening, speaking and writing) are part of the end product and are also a tool for introducing new language and practising and checking linguistic knowledge. In the content classroom the four skills are a means of learning new information and displaying an understanding of the subject being taught. So the language is a means to an end, rather than an end in itself, and the structure and style of the language is often less colloquial and more complex.

CLIL takes place in a number of different teaching situations. It may be more useful to think of it as being on a continuum from total to partial immersion. There is a minority of schools and institutions where all subjects are taught through a foreign language all the time, for example, in some universities and in International Schools. More usually, some subjects are taught through a foreign language some of the time. What seems to be universal is that the practice of teaching a subject through another language is becoming more and more common, and this inevitably leads to yet another challenge for a number of teachers. Unfortunately the push for CLIL has been faster than the training for the teachers who are required to deliver it. Many subject and language teachers suddenly find themselves having to teach a subject through English without the support or training they need.

There are two different types of teachers involved in CLIL, who have very different needs—the expertise of the language teacher may not be shared by the content teacher and vice versa.

1 Teachers of English who now have to teach another subject through English, rather than just teaching the language. Their problem is usually the content—the subject matter. In fact many of them have studied subjects other than English as part of their degree, but they may not be up-to-date with the current syllabus. However, teaching through English is not the main problem for them and they have the advantage of being able to communicate in the classroom with more confidence.

2   Subject teachers who now have to teach their subject through English. These teachers know the subject matter but may lack experience and confidence in two particular areas:
- their own command of the language may naturally be limited. They are not used to giving input through another language, or to helping their students with the language. This certainly affects their confidence as well as their ability;
- as subject teachers they may not have the armoury of interactive activities that language teachers need. Language learning is by its very nature dependent on interactive communication. When teaching a subject in the mother tongue, the need for repetition, checking of understanding, and active learning is not as crucial as it is in language teaching.

The advantages and challenges of CLIL

There are a number of claims made for the advantages of CLIL, although it is difficult to substantiate them. One is that it can develop foreign language ability more effectively than conventional foreign language teaching does. What it certainly can do is to prepare students for future study and the workplace where they are likely to need to operate in English.

An advantage for language teachers is that the content is ready-made. This takes away the need to spend a lot of time thinking up topics that work and engage the students. It is also likely that the students are more motivated when they are learning through English something that is part of their school learning and thinking, rather than just learning the language, which may or may not seem to them to have any obvious purpose. Only a minority of young people have an interest in words for their own sake. In CLIL the language is very clearly a means to an end. Many children now start learning English at a very young age so that when they reach secondary school they do not want to repeat the same language lessons.

The research done by Howard Gardner into multiple intelligences is highly relevant here. (For more information about multiple intelligences see Appendix 3.) When we are teaching another subject through a foreign language it is likely that we will draw on more of the intelligences and this is likely to be helpful to our learners. The linguistic intelligence, which is prevalent in language teaching, is supported by the intelligences required for particular subjects so that, for example, the musical, kinaesthetic, and logical/mathematical intelligences are on a more equal footing.

However, CLIL certainly does present some problems for both the teacher and the learners. When working with subject and language teachers who teach subjects through English we often hear cries such as these:
- It's so difficult for me to explain in English.
- My students don't like listening to English.
- My students find it hard to read in English.
- I have to write most of my own materials.

- The book I've got is so boring.
- I can't get my students to participate in English.

In language teaching it is important to encourage and devote time to students **producing** the language rather than just learning **about** it in terms of its grammar and structure. This means that lessons are often highly interactive with students trying out various tasks in the new language. Language teachers are encouraged to reduce their talking time in order to allow for more student talking time. In subject teaching on the other hand it is important for students to take in and understand the curriculum. There may be a lot of facts and information for them to learn and the input may be highly complex. In order to cover the curriculum a teacher must devote more time to giving input and not necessarily allow so much time for the students to give output or to be interactive; in fact, there needs to be more teacher talking time. Subject teachers teaching through another language may have a language problem, so they need to use strategies which reduce the time spent addressing the class from the front.

In the same way, it is important for language teachers teaching a subject to use interactive activities which help the learners understand and engage their interest. If we teach a subject which students find difficult, boring or unappealing, and if on top of that, the students are being taught in a language they find difficult, then for them to learn anything is going to be a miracle. Our only hope is to make the lessons active and interesting, that is, the activities and processes must be appealing so as to counterbalance any negative aspects of the content and language. This book aims to address this need.

The aims of this book

This book aims to support CLIL teachers and suggest solutions to some of their problems. There are not as yet many books written specifically to teach a particular subject through another language. This is why the methodology in subject books does not take into account the language element of CLIL. This book is meant to be a support to the subject book. It is a book of classroom activities that can be used when teaching any subject. It offers you ideas to create stimulating and varied lessons, working with groups, pairs, whole classes, and mixed-ability classes. Our purpose is to provide activities which will help you make your subject matter more easily understood, and take the pressure off you in terms of your own language skills by reducing the language obstacle for you and your learners. These strategies will reduce your need to speak in front of the whole class. This will enable you to use the materials you have more effectively, and at the same time, should reduce your stress levels.

CLIL methodology

In conventional foreign language teaching, the key features are usually controlled input and practice of language points. In teaching a subject through a foreign language the methodology is different. As the subject dictates the language demands, we have to analyse the language demands of a given lesson and give the learners the language support which they need. Learners will need help in the areas of lexis, cognitive functions and study skills.

At the lower grades the emphasis is likely to be more on receptive than productive skills. However, learners will also need to write and to speak in the foreign language and will need support and help to do this. At lower levels the writing component could just be copy writing and labelling objects, or writing one-word answers to questions. What these learners will not want to do, or be able to do, is to listen and read for extended periods of time without being actively involved. We need to give them short bursts of comprehensible input.

It is clear that in CLIL we have to include more strategies to support understanding and learning. One such strategy would be to use visuals such as pictures, charts and diagrams. Another is to plan lessons to support the language and learning needs, for example, providing a chart to fill in to accompany a reading text, or a framework for a writing activity, identifying key vocabulary, and varying the activities to include whole-class, small-group, pair and individual work. There also needs to be a lot of repetition and consolidation. For example, a writing activity may need to be done twice so that the second time the students have the opportunity to focus more on the language.

There is no reason to abandon the use of the mother tongue where it can be used as a support and learning tool. A good example would be group work in which students could discuss a problem or piece of information in their mother tongue as a route to achieving the given task in English. In reality a lot of code-switching—moving between the two languages—will take place and that is perfectly natural, particularly in the lower grades. This book offers a number of activities which include the optional use of the mother tongue.

Assessment is a thorny problem for CLIL and this book does not go into this area. However, it seems to us to be important that weighting is given to both the subject and the language. What that ratio should be may depend on the age and level of the learners. In some cases it may be more appropriate to evaluate the language and the content separately. In this case the assessment of the content could be in the mother tongue, or if in the foreign language, could use non-verbal responses. A personal learning portfolio is one way for students to notice and think about their progress and needs, and this should cover both content and language.

How to use this book

This is a book you can dip into when you feel the need to adapt, clarify, simplify or liven up the methodology in your coursebook.

How the book is organized

The main core of the book consists of classroom activities which can be used to teach any subject. In the final section of this introduction there is guidance as to how to adapt, simplify or modify an activity. This book provides the process; your subject book provides the content.

   The activities are divided into the following chapters, though some activities could appear in more than one chapter.

1 Giving new information (listening and reading)
2 Teaching and activating key vocabulary
3 Speaking
4 Writing
5 Consolidation and revision
6 Using supplementary resources
7 Project work

Appendix 1: Language to help you in the classroom

This is a useful reference section for you when planning your classroom instructions as it includes the language you will need to set up the activities in this book.

Appendix 2: Useful language for students

This is a short reference section of language for different cognitive functions, for example, hypothesizing, defining, cause and effect, evaluating. Refer to this for the language you may need to pre-teach.

Appendix 3: Useful books

Appendix 4: Useful websites

This covers different subjects.

How each activity is organized

Each activity is organized under the following headings:

Aims

These are headed 'Language' and 'Other'. The language aims signpost the language skills the students will need to carry out the activity. Appendix 2 provides some help for this. Under 'Other' we have included more general aims, plus any study skills involved.

Demo subject

Each activity is described using a demo subject, but it is important to realise that the activity could be used for other subjects just by changing the content. For each demo subject we give a specific topic, for example, Chemistry—Topic: The Periodic Table. The demo subjects in this book cover the following subjects:

Mathematics, Biology, Chemistry, Physics, Environmental Studies, Food Technology, History, Geography, Literature, Sports Science and Physical Education, Art, Music, ICT, Business Studies, Design and Technology, Religious Studies and PSHE (Personal, Social and Health Education).

Materials

Some activities require no materials, others require some. We suggest that you make your materials recyclable!

Alternative subjects

For each activity we give three examples, trying to cover a mix of sciences, humanities, arts, and more practical subjects. However, there are many other subjects that the activity could be applied to.

Preparation

This describes any work you have to do before the lesson. Some of the activities do not require any preparation.

Procedure

This gives step-by-step details of how to teach the activity.

There are two headings we cannot include:

a Level—We cannot identify this as it will depend on the content and topic you are using. The processes themselves could be used at any level. However, the activities are designed for students aged 11–18 so we have assumed that in terms of language level the learners will not be beginners.

b Time—This will depend on the content you use, the ability of the students, the size of the class and your lesson objectives. Some of the activities could be spread over more than one lesson or some steps could be done for homework.

How to use and modify an activity

Your starting point is your content and aim. If you look in the relevant chapter you can apply your content to the activities there. When teaching a subject your content is a given, so you can use these activities to get across the content you already have. For example, you may want to consolidate some previously taught content. Look in Chapter 5, 'Consolidation and revision', where you will find activities that you can use with your specific content.

Do not be put off using an activity if it does not mention your subject. It is impossible for us to include examples for each activity for about twenty different subjects! However, we have tried to make the activities as easy to generalize as possible so that you could use them with the content that you need. To demonstrate this we describe an activity which uses content for a higher language level. Of course, this activity may not be at the level that you need, and our demo subject may not be the subject that you teach. For this reason we will follow it with examples of how to do the following:

A simplify the text
B make the text more visual
C analyse the language support your students need
D adapt the activity to a different subject

Here is a detailed example of how this might be done:

Guess the answer

Aims	LANGUAGE	Writing questions; giving short answers.
	OTHER	Reading or listening; scanning and predicting.
Demo subject	PHYSICS	
	TOPIC	Conduction and convection
Alternative subjects	MUSIC	Different genres of music
	HISTORY	The Aztecs
	SPORTS SCIENCE	Sports related injuries

Any subject your students need to know about.

Preparation

1 Write or choose a text from a book on the topic you want to teach.

2 Write or choose a set of questions that are answered in the text. These could be the questions provided in your book.

Example   **Procedure**

1 Write the topic of the text on the board.

Conduction and convection

If things are left to their own devices heat transfer is always from hot to cool and heat energy always travels from the hot object to the cooler object. Heat transfer like this only happens when there is a difference in temperature.

The particles that make up a hot object have more energy than the particles that make up a cold object. If the hot particles get the chance, they will pass on their energy to colder particles. This process is called conduction. Particles which are close to each other pass heat energy from the hot particles to the cold particles. Conduction happens best in solids as the particles are close together. It also happens in liquids but to a lesser extent, and hardly at all in gases.

Heat energy can also be transferred from one place to another by convection. Convection is different from conduction because the particles in the substance actually move taking the heat energy with them. They do not pass on the heat energy as in conduction. It should be easy to see that convection happens most easily in liquids and gases where the particles can move around much more freely than in a solid. Heated particles within a liquid or gas always rise taking the heat energy with them.

Possible questions

1   In which direction does heat transfer—from cool to hot or from hot to cool?

2   In which matter are the particles close together?

3   Which is the most likely matter for conduction—a solid, a liquid or a gas?

4   Which is the most likely matter for convection—solids or liquids?

5   What is the difference between conduction and convection?

2   Tell the students you are going ask them questions related to a text that they have not seen yet. They must **not** write down the questions. However, they must guess the answer to each one and write it down. They do not have to write whole sentences. Point out that it does not matter if they guess wrongly—this process is just to get them thinking. They may discuss questions with a partner.

3   Read out the questions and give the students time to write their answers.

4   As a whole class, or in pairs, they compare their answers. Then they re-formulate the original questions and write them down, leaving a space after each one for the answer. Check their questions.

5 Read the text, or give them the text to read themselves to check their answers. They write down the correct answers, individually or in pairs.

6 Check their answers.

Comments

If step 5 is done as a reading it could be a homework activity.

Acknowledgements

Information taken from www.digitalbrain.com.

A Simplifying the text

Some possible strategies:
- shorten by removing any redundancies
- shorten by removing any unnecessary information
- shorten sentences into simple structures
- replace more complicated lexis
- avoid passive voice
- avoid idiomatic expressions
- avoid phrasal verbs

Example

> ## Conduction and convection (simplified text)
>
> Heat transfer is always from hot to cool. Heat energy always travels from the hot object to the cooler object. Heat transfer like this only happens when there is a difference in temperature.
>
> The particles in a hot object have more energy than the particles in a cold object. Hot particles can pass on their energy to colder particles. This process is called conduction. Particles which are close to each other pass on heat energy from the hot particles to the cold particles. Conduction happens best in solids as the particles are close together. It happens less in liquids, and almost never in gases.
>
> Heat energy can also transfer from one place to another by a process called convection. Convection is different from conduction because the particles actually move taking the heat energy with them. They do not pass on the heat energy as in conduction. Convection happens most easily in liquids and gases, where the particles can move around much more freely than in a solid. Heated particles within a liquid or gas always rise taking the heat energy with them.

B Making the text more visual

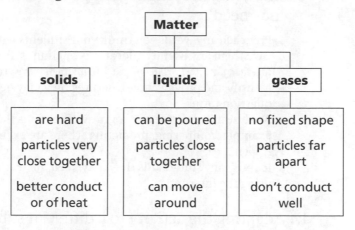

Matter		
solids	**liquids**	**gases**
are hard	can be poured	no fixed shape
particles very close together	particles close together	particles far apart
better conduct or of heat	can move around	don't conduct well

Conduction
- hot particles pass on heat energy to colder particles
- solids are the better conductors of heat energy
- particles are in rows and very close together so they can't move around.

Particles in solids

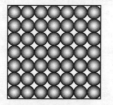

Convection
- heated particles rise and take energy with them
- particles are further apart so they can move around

Particles in liquids   **Particles in gases**

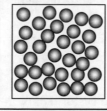   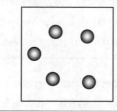

Show students the visuals before step 5 on page 14, i.e. before they read the original text.

When asking the questions you could help them by writing the keywords on the board.

Example 1 cool to hot?
2 solids, liquids, gases

C Analysing the language support your students may need

- Pre-teach any words you think your students will not know.
- Give them any useful collocations or chunks, for example, *close together, far apart, from one place to another, move around freely*.
- Identify and provide any structures they may need: in this case, question forms.
- Analyze and practise any cognitive functions they may need, for example, comparing, predicting. There are examples of these in Appendix 2.
- Identify any study skills they may need, for example, scanning or using the internet.

D Adapting the activity to a different subject

Subject **History**

The Aztecs

The Aztec people established a vast empire in central and southern Mexico. They were there from the 14th century AD/CE. The name 'Aztec' came from a mythical place to the north called Azatlán, but they also called themselves Mexica. A central part of the Aztec religion was to offer human and animal sacrifices. The highest honour for warriors was to offer themselves as a human sacrifice, or to die in battle. It is believed that the Aztecs used the fruit of the cacao tree to make delicious chocolate. In the 16th century the Spanish, led by Hernan Cortéz, invaded and destroyed their empire. The leader of the Aztecs at this time was the Great Montezuma II.

Questions

1 Where did the Aztec people live?
2 In which centuries did the Aztec empire exist?
3 Why did they offer human and animal sacrifices?
4 What delicious food did they discover?
5 Which country invaded and destroyed their empire?

Acknowledgements

Text adapted from www.SchoolHistory.co.uk.

1

Giving new information

The activities in this chapter can be used whenever you need to give new information. They focus on getting away from the teacher-led method of giving information. This makes life easier for you and for the learners. When taking in complicated information in another language, students need to be given help to understand the important concepts. They need to be actively involved and given tasks which will enhance their understanding. This means they have to 'work for' the information rather than trying to take it in passively.

The activities in this chapter are a mixture of reading and listening tasks. There is even one non-verbal task, 1.10, 'Correct me'. Some of the listening tasks, such as 1.13, 'ABC dictations', and 1.14, 'Mutual dictations', involve active dictations.

We have included a number of different strategies and study skills which the students need to develop.

- Note-taking, as in 1.4, 'Co-operative listening'.
- Scanning, as in 1.5, 'Scan the text', 1.6, 'Write the text question'.
- Ordering, as in 1.7, 'Text circles', 1.8, 'Getting the right order'.
- Using the mother tongue as in 1.15, 'Spot the sentence'.
- Repetition, as in 1.11, 'Parroting', 1.12, 'Echoing'.
- Focusing on key words, as in 1.2, 'Listening with key words', 1.3, 'Understanding textbook language'.
- Cooperative learning, as in 1.12, 'Echoing', 1.13, 'ABC dictation'.
- Predicting, as in 1.6, 'Write the text question', 1.10, 'Correct me'.

Many of the activities in this section also lead into an output stage where the students write or speak about the new input they have been given.

1.1 Ask me your questions

Aims   LANGUAGE   Asking *wh-* questions (see Appendix 2).

         OTHER   Giving students a voice; arousing students' curiosity; listening for specific information.

Demo subject   ART

       TOPIC   Pablo Picasso

Alternative subjects FOOD TECHNOLOGY Bacteria in food

MATHEMATICS Pythagoras' theorem

DESIGN AND TECHNOLOGY Plastics

Any new information you need to teach

Preparation

Prepare an outline of the information you want to give your students.

Procedure

1 Remind the students about question forms by practising *yes/no* and *wh-* questions. In this example the questions are in the past. Write examples on the board. (See the example below.)

2 Write the topic of your outline on the board.

3 Put the students into pairs. Give them a time limit (about 7 minutes) to tell each other what they know about the topic and then to write a question about it that they want answered. They write their questions on the board. Correct any mistakes. If necessary they write their questions in the mother tongue. You then help them translate the questions into English.

Example **Possible student questions:**

Pablo Picasso

What nationality was he?
Did he have children?
When did he live?
Where did he live?
What materials did he use?
What is the name of his most famous painting?

4 The class copy all the questions on the board into their notebooks.

5 Each student who wrote a question says it out loud to the class. The class try to answer it.

6 Tell the students you are going to give them a talk. While they are listening they should tick any of the questions they think you have answered.

7 Give your talk, incorporating as many answers to their questions as possible or sensible.

8 When you have finished, invite any students who think their question has been answered to give the answer. If they are right, they come to the board and rub off their question.

9 Ask pairs to work with another pair. They go through the questions in their notebooks and answer any they can.

10 Check their answers.

11 Go through any questions still left on the board and either answer them on the spot, or save them for another lesson. Alternatively, ask the students to find the answers for their homework.

1.2 Listening with key words

Aims LANGUAGE Re-creating a text; understanding key words; listening for key words; practising writing.

OTHER Working in groups.

Materials Coloured card or paper.

Demo subject DESIGN AND TECHNOLOGY

TOPIC Plastics

Alternative subjects PHYSICS Properties of light

FOOD TECHNOLOGY Food safety and hygiene

HISTORY The slave trade

Any text your students need to understand

Preparation

1 Select a text which contains important factual information. This could be from the coursebook. Either record it, or use it as a dictation.

2 Write a list of several key words or phrases from the text and photocopy enough copies for pairs or small groups of students. Mount the copies on different coloured paper or card and then cut them up so there is one key word or phrase on each slip.

Example

> ## Plastics
>
> Plastics are man-made materials. Plastics have taken the place of traditional materials like woods and metals.
>
> Plastics differ from other materials largely because of the size of their molecules. Most materials have molecules made up of fewer than 300 atoms. Plastics contain thousands of atoms. We call them macromolecules.
>
> Some plastics are derived from natural substances such as animals, insects and plants but most are man-made. These are named synthetic plastics.
>
> Most synthetic plastics come from crude oil but coal and natural gas are also used.
>
> When crude oil is refined, gases are given off. The gases are broken down into monomers. These are chemical substances consisting of a single molecule. Thousands of these are linked together in a process called polymerisation to form new compounds called polymers.

> ## Key words and phrases
>
> | | | |
> |---|---|---|
> | man-made materials | take the place of | refined |
> | fewer than 300 atoms | macromolecules | derived from |
> | natural substances | synthetic plastics | crude oil |
> | monomers | compounds called polymers | |

Procedure

1 Put the students into groups of not more than four.

2 Give each group a set of the key words and phrases and tell them these are taken from the text they are about to hear. Give students time to read and help each other understand them. They can ask you for help and use dictionaries.

3 Tell the students in each group to share out the slips. While you read out the text they must place the key words in the order in which they hear them. They may hear some words twice but they place the card the first time they hear a word.

4 Let them send a 'spy' to the other groups to compare their order. Read or play the text again.

5 In their groups they use their ordered key words to help them write the text from memory. This does not have to be word for word as the original.

6 Read or play the text again.

7 Give students time to edit their texts before taking them in for marking.

8 Give the students a copy of the original text, or direct them to the appropriate page of the coursebook.

Variation

This could be a student-generated activity.

1 Give different groups or pairs a different text.

2 The students select their own key words and write them on different slips of paper.

3 Combine two groups or pairs. They take turns to read their texts while the others order the key words.

Acknowledgements

Text taken from www.design-technology.org.

1.3 Understanding textbook language

Aims LANGUAGE Learning technical terms; recognizing and learning key expressions; getting and sharing new information; becoming familiar with a more formal academic style of writing; building up an unseen text.

Materials Overhead projector or screen.

Demo subject BUSINESS STUDIES

TOPIC The factors of production

Alternative subjects GEOGRAPHY Settlements in MEDCS (More Economically Developed Countries) and LEDCS (Less Economically Developed Countries).

PHYSICS Evolution—The life of a star

Vocabulary for any subject

Preparation

1 Find a text which has key words to be learnt and expressions you want the students to recognize and practise.

2 Write the complete text on OHT.

3 Make a duplicated gapped text for each student. Make the gaps big enough to write in the missing words or letters.

4 List the key words and more formal expressions you want your students to learn.

Example

There are four main factors of production, known as resources, that are used to produce the economy's goods and services. These are land, labour, capital, and enterprise. All businesses need land to create their products. Businesses may use the land as in agriculture, build on it, extract raw materials from it, or rent or buy it for their factories, offices, and warehouses. Businesses employ people to make and market their products: this is the labour. Businesses need to invest money in machinery, equipment, and building; this investment is called capital. The entrepreneur owns the business and takes the chance that his or her product will be a success; these people are also known as risk-takers.

Th＿＿＿ are f＿＿r ma＿＿ ＿act＿＿＿ of pro＿＿＿＿＿＿＿, kn＿＿n as ＿＿＿our＿＿＿, that are u＿＿＿ to produ＿＿ the ec＿n＿my's go＿＿＿ and ＿＿＿vices. These are l＿＿＿ , labour, c＿＿＿＿＿＿＿, and e＿＿＿＿＿＿＿＿ . All businesses n＿＿＿ l＿＿d to cre＿＿＿ their products. Businesses may use the l＿＿＿ as in agricul＿＿＿＿, build on it, ex＿＿＿＿＿＿ r＿＿ materials from it, or re＿＿ or buy it for their fact＿＿＿＿＿, offices, and wa＿＿＿＿＿＿＿＿. Businesses em＿＿＿＿ people to make and m＿＿＿＿＿ their products: this is the la＿＿＿＿. Businesses n＿＿＿ t＿ inv＿＿＿ money in machinery, equ＿＿＿＿＿＿＿, and buildings; this invest＿＿＿＿ is ca＿＿＿＿ cap＿＿＿＿. The entrepreneur owns the business and t＿＿＿＿ the ch＿＿＿＿ that his or her pro＿＿＿＿ will be a success; these people are al＿＿ k＿＿＿＿ as risk-takers.

Key words and expressions

resources   produce   goods and services   labour   capital
enterprise   extract   raw materials   rent   warehouses
invest   main factors   known as   are used to   to create
as in   need to   is called

Procedure

1   Write the title of the text on the board. Tell the students that you are going to read the text to them.

2   Ask the students to work in pairs to write a list of key words and phrases they think could be in the text. Divide the board in half and ask the students to read out their words. Write these on one side of the board. Add and explain any new words from your key word list that are not on the board.

3   Write the list of expressions on the other side of the board and explain that more formal expressions are often used in textbooks. Discuss the expressions and translate into the mother tongue.

4   Read the text. Ask the students to listen but not write anything down.

5   Read the text twice more. Now tell the students to write down any of the words and phrases they hear while you are reading, but **not** to make notes about the text.

6   When you have finished reading put students into groups of four. Give the groups time to compare their individual lists.

7   Give every student a copy of the gapped text. Tell the students they can work together to build up the text. Explain that they can send members of their group to ask other groups for help, **but they must not ask you for help**. Give the students time to work on the text.

8   Stop the activity just before the groups have completed the whole text.

9   The students take it in turns to read out their texts. When they have a gap they nominate someone from another group to continue. If nobody knows the missing word give them clues such as *it's the opposite of…, it means the same as…, another word for this could be…*.

10 Show the completed text on the OHP or screen for a final check. Ask students to write down the key words and expressions from the text and take it in turns to explain them to their partners.

Follow-up

Ask the students to write sentences using the expressions from the board as homework.

Acknowledgements

Example text adapted from *Business Studies,* David Floyd, Letts GCSE Visual Revision Guides.

1.4 Co-operative listening

Aims LANGUAGE Listening.

OTHER Note-taking; cooperative learning.

Subject Any

Preparation

1 Prepare and practise reading aloud a short talk on the topic you want to tell your students about.

Procedure

1 If you have a large class call the front row A and the row behind them B. Repeat this sequence with the remaining rows. If you have a small class arrange them into one A row with one B row sitting behind them. All the students must be facing you.

2 Write the topic of your talk on the board.

3 Tell the class that you are going to give them a short talk. The A rows are the listeners and must not write anything down. The B rows are the writers and can take as many notes as they like.

4 Give half your talk.

5 When you have finished tell the A rows to turn their chairs round to face their group B partners. The As tell the Bs what they can remember from listening to the talk. The Bs listen carefully and use their notes to jog the As' memories. They need to help the As to remember more, but they must not just read out all their notes.

6 Now ask the students to change roles so that the As are the writers and the Bs are the listeners. Give the rest of your talk. Repeat step 5 with Bs recalling what they heard, helped by the As from their notes.

7 Working in their pairs they now reconstruct the notes so that they will be a useful reference.

8 When they have finished ask them to discuss the difference between listening and taking notes, and listening without taking notes. What are the advantages and disadvantages of each?

Comments

It is all too easy to get into the mode of mindless note-taking. Some students love taking notes and others do not. We are all different but sometimes it is useful to try another method to check that what we are doing is really helping us.

Acknowledgments

This activity is adapted from an idea from Simon Marshall.

1.5 Scan the text

Aims   **LANGUAGE**   Reporting back; introducing a text; giving input; skimming and scanning; making long texts less stressful; translating.

         OTHER   Working in groups.

Materials   Slips of paper—one for each search section.

Demo subject   **SPORTS SCIENCE**

         TOPIC   Aerobic training

Alternative subjects   **LITERATURE**   Epic poetry

         BUSINESS STUDIES   Company reports

         PHYSICS   Detailed text about nuclear power

Preparation

1   Find a text and make sure each student has a copy. Keep a note of the source for the students.

2   Identify the key points you want your students to remember and write these down as a list (see example below) in English or the mother tongue, or a mixture of the two.

Example

Key points list
1 An aerobically fit individual can work longer, more vigorously, and achieve a quicker recovery.
2 What factors affect aerobic training? Frequency, duration and intensity.
3 The Karvonen Formula calculates your heart rate reserve range.
4 _____ if you find it difficult to say a few words, you are probably working out anaerobically.
5 For a good indication of aerobic exercise, you should be able to say a few words, catch your breath, and then carry on talking.
6 Aerobic exercise strengthens the heart and lungs (cardio-vascular system).
7 If you are talking all the way through your workout, it's _____ .

Photocopiable © Oxford University Press

3   Write each sentence or sentence part on a separate slip of paper. Remove the numbering. Mix the slips up so that they do not follow the order of the text.

Procedure

1   Put the students into groups of three or four. Give a copy of the text to each student.

2   Tell them that one person at a time from each group will be the messenger who walks out to you and reads the slip of paper you show them. The messenger holds the information in their head and goes back and tells their group what they read. If the slip is in the mother tongue the group must translate it into English.

3   The group then scan the text until they find the sentence or sentence part that was on your slip of paper. They number and underline it on their text.

4   New messengers go to you and repeat the activity until all the search slips have been used. Keep up a reasonable pace, and encourage the students to work quickly by saying, for example:
    I'm about to show the next slip.
    As quickly as you can, please.
    Which groups are ready for the next?
    OK, next one coming up.

5   Now read out the beginning of any slip and choose a student to say the rest of the sentence.

6   Take the texts away and ask the groups to write down everything they can remember. They may remember only the key words on the slips. This sets the key words in their minds.

7   Give the texts back to the students for them to file and use as a reference.

Variation

You can use pictures, diagrams, charts, and graphs in place of words on the slips to represent particular sentences or parts of sentences.

Acknowledgements

Text adapted from www.netfit.co.uk.

1.6 Write the text question

Aims LANGUAGE Giving examples (see Appendix 2); predicting (see Appendix 2).

OTHER Reading and selecting key information; understanding written examination questions; note-taking.

Materials Eight large cards—one for each section title; sheets of paper—one for each student; slips of paper (optional).

Demo subject FOOD TECHNOLOGY

TOPIC Food preservation

Alternative subjects PHYSICS Properties of matter

DESIGN AND TECHNOLOGY Health and safety in the workplace

RELIGIOUS STUDIES The Sikh nation

Any subject your students need

Preparation

1 Find a suitable text.

2 Make two copies of the complete text. Keep one complete copy for yourself and divide the other copy into logical sections. Photocopy each of the sections three times.

With this topic the sections could be:

(a) Refrigeration and freezing, (b) Canning, (c) Dehydration, (d) Freeze-drying, (e) Salting, Pickling, (f) Pasteurising, Fermenting, and Carbonating, (g) Chemical preservation, and (h) Irradiation.

3 Write the section titles, for example, 'Canning', 'Irradiation', on the large cards in large print. Paste or staple the text sections on the cards, with three cards for each text section, for example, three copies of the 'Irradiation text', and so on. This is to make it easy for groups of students to have room to stand and read the texts. Pin the sections up under the appropriate title.

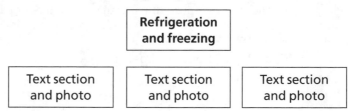

Procedure

1 Write the title, 'How food preservation works', on the board. Write the same title in the mother tongue under it. Get the students to suggest as many areas of the subject as possible, for example, refrigeration, pickling, canning. Write these on the board. If students use their mother tongue, write the English equivalents underneath. Then add from your original list any the students have not mentioned.

Example

How food preservation works

Refrigeration and freezing are probably the most popular forms of food preservation in use today. In the case of refrigeration, the idea is to **slow bacterial action** to a crawl so that it takes food much longer (perhaps a week or two, rather than half a day) to spoil. In the case of freezing, the idea is to **stop bacterial action** altogether. Frozen bacteria are completely inactive.

A bag of frozen vegetables will last many months without spoiling.

Refrigeration and freezing are used on almost all foods: meats, fruits, vegetables, beverages, etc. In general, refrigeration has no effect on a food's taste or texture. Freezing has no effect on the taste or texture of most meats, has minimal effects on vegetables, but often completely changes fruits (which become mushy). Refrigeration's minimal effects account for its wide popularity.

2 Give each student a sheet of paper and tell them to fold it into three parts horizontally. At the top of the first section ask them to write 'Things I knew'; at the top of the second section they write 'Things I didn't know'; and on the third they write 'Examples to remember'. Put the students into groups with a maximum of six.

3 Tell each group which text section to read. Explain that you will give them a time limit.

4 Ask the students to go and read the text. They do this individually. As they read, each student writes down information under the three headings on their paper. They may make quick drawings or notes for the 'Examples to remember' section.

5 When the time limit is up ask the students to return to their groups and pool their information.

6 Each group presents their information to the rest of the class.

Example *These are the things most of the group knew…*
Things some of us didn't know were…
An example of this is…

While each group is presenting, the others make notes.

7 This step is optional depending on the course. The groups write possible examination questions about their text area on slips of paper—one slip per question. The groups display these questions by the appropriate texts. Give the students time to move from text to text and write down some or all of the possible questions.

8 Give the students the reference you used so that they can read the whole text later. Alternatively, you can give a copy to each student.

Acknowledgements

Text taken from 'How food preservation works', by Marshall Brain, found on www.howstuffworks.com.

1.7 Text circles

Aims LANGUAGE **Asking and answering questions (see Appendix 2); ordering words.**

OTHER **Getting new information; working in groups; reading.**

Materials **Sheets of paper for the prepared text extracts.**

Demo subject SCIENCE

TOPIC **Making copper chloride**

Alternative subjects PSHE **How the European Parliament works**

MUSIC **Jamaican music**

DESIGN AND TECHNOLOGY **Shaping plastics—injection and extrusion**

Vocabulary for any subject

Preparation

1 Find or write a short text.

Example

This is how we get copper chloride to crystallize. First of all add copper carbonate to a jar containing hydrochloric acid. Wait until the fizzing stops. Then filter the solution through filter paper into a flask. This removes the unreacted copper carbonate and gives a copper chloride solution. The next thing to do is to pour the copper chloride solution into an evaporating dish. Put the dish on top of a beaker which has some water in it. Place the beaker on a tripod and heat it until the first crystals begin to appear. Remove the heat and leave the solution for a few days for the copper chloride to crystallize.

2 Divide the text into sections, making sure that each section break is in the middle of the sentence. (See the example below). There should be enough parts for each student in a group to have one. Type or write the prepared text in the parts, writing the number 1 next to the beginning. Do **not** write any other numbers.

Example

1 This is how we get copper chloride to crystallize. First of all add copper carbonate to a jar containing hydrochloric acid. Wait until the
fizzing stops. Then filter the solution through filter paper into a flask. This removes the unreacted copper carbonate and gives
a copper chloride solution. The next thing to do is to pour the copper chloride solution into an evaporating dish. Put the dish on top
of a beaker which has some water in it. Place the beaker on a tripod and heat it until the first crystals begin to
appear. Remove the heat and leave the solution for a few days for the copper chloride to crystallize.

3 Cut into slips. In the example above you have five slips for one circle of five students. Duplicate enough sets of five slips for the class.

Procedure

1 Write the text title on the board. Write up any difficult words or phrases from the text and give the translation in the mother tongue. Ask students to listen and repeat the English.

2 Tell them to get into circles of five. Give out the slips. Ask students to read their slips to each other. They must keep their own slips of paper. Tell them that the student with slip number 1 has the beginning of the text. Ask them to work out the correct order of the text and to stand in that order.

3 Ask the students who have the first part of the text to read out their slips. Then get the rest of the group to read their slips in their chosen order to check that they are correct. They do this in their groups.

4 Choose a group to read out their text in their chosen order. The whole class listens and checks. Do this with another group to give them time to check, hold and anchor the information in their minds.

5 Take in the slips. Give out copies of the text, one for each student.

6 The students sit down. Each student writes a question about the text.

7 Taking their questions with them the students move round the class asking and answering the questions.

Variation

Use two different texts covering a similar topic. Use different coloured paper for each text. Alternatively use different fonts. Each student should have a copy of both texts.

1.8 Getting the right order

Aims   LANGUAGE Adverbs of sequence, for example, *after*, *before*, *then* (see Appendix 2).

OTHER   Memorizing a sequence of steps; using the kinaesthetic intelligence.

Materials One slip of paper per student.

Demo subject LITERATURE

TOPIC Periods of literature

Alternative subjects SCIENCES The steps involved in an experiment

HISTORY The order of events, monarchs, battles

MATHEMATICS The steps to solve a specific calculation

Any subject which involves a sequence or order

Preparation

Write out the steps of the sequence you want your students to learn.

Procedure

1 Show on the board the steps you want your students to memorize. Number them. Give the students time to try to memorize the correct order.

Example Periods of Literature

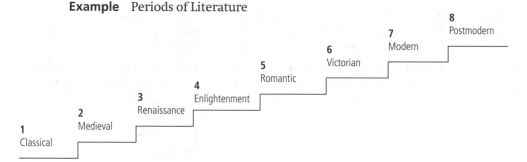

2 Put students into groups of the same number as the steps that you want them to memorize. In this example they will be groups of eight. Number the students 1–8. If you have more than eight students in a group two can share a number. If you have seven students, you can give one student two consecutive numbers.

3 Student 1 in the group stands and says the name of the first step, student 2 the second and so on. Check each group. If a student makes a mistake, student 1 starts again from the beginning. They continue like this until they have managed to get through the whole sequence at least twice without making a mistake.

4 Ask the students to write the name of their step on a piece of paper. They mix them up and each student in the group takes one.

5 This time they must stand and say the step on their piece of paper at the appropriate time.

6 Repeat step 5 as often as necessary, getting the students to re-distribute the slips each time.

7 Ask the students to write the different periods on a staircase in their books.

1.9 Students as words

Aims LANGUAGE Spatial language (see Appendix 2).

OTHER Reading; gap-filling; using the kinaesthetic intelligence; using charts or diagrams.

Materials Two sets of slips of paper; an overhead projector or electronic whiteboard.

Demo subject MUSIC

TOPIC The orchestra

Alternative subjects HISTORY An historical family tree: the names of the characters and events

BIOLOGY The human skeleton: different bones of the human body and parts of the body related to the bones

MATHEMATICS Pictures of different shapes: the names of the different shapes and words connected to the different shapes

Preparation

1 Find or write a text which includes information about two sub-topics. In the example on the next page the topic is 'The orchestra', with the sub-topics being the instruments in the sections of the orchestra and how the orchestra is arranged.

2 Photocopy one text per student or pair of students, or project it onto a screen.

3 Make a gapped version of the text and photocopy it for each student.

4 Draw a blank chart of the different sections of the orchestra. Put it on the board for the students to copy or project it onto a screen.

5 Make Group A slips of paper with the names of the different sections of the orchestra. Group A will be approximately one third of the class.

6 Make Group B slips of paper with the names of the different musical instruments. They can be duplicated so that everyone gets one. Group B will be approximately two-thirds of the class. Make sure you have at least one instrument to match each section of the orchestra. If you have a large class instruments can be duplicated.

Example

The orchestra sits in a semi-circular arrangement with the conductor facing them at the front, with his or her back to the audience. The largest section is the string section, which includes the violins, violas, cellos and double bass.

The first violins are on the conductor's left with the second violins in the next triangle. The violas are immediately in front of the conductor and the cellos are on the right of the conductor in front of the double basses.

The next biggest section is the woodwind section. The flute section is behind the violas, next to the second violins, and the oboes are next to them. The clarinets are behind the flutes, with the bassoons behind the oboes.

The brass section comprises French horns, trumpets, trombones and tubas. They sit behind the woodwind section with the French horns behind the clarinets, the trumpets in the middle and the trombones and tubas together on the right.

The percussion section is across the middle at the back.

If a harp is needed it goes on the left of the conductor at the back of the first violins.

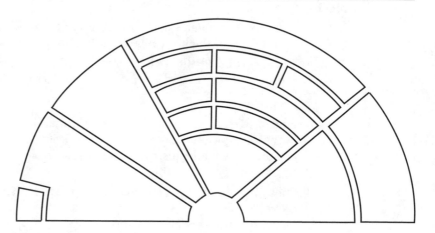

Procedure

1   Ask the class to read the text. Give them an appropriate time limit to take it in.

2   Divide the class into Group A (approximately one-third of the class) and Group B (two-thirds). Take away the text from Group A.

3   Give out the slips of paper with the names of the sections of the orchestra to the students in Group A. There must be at least one student per slip.

4   Show the blank orchestra chart on the board or the screen.

5   Tell Group A to position themselves according to their place on the chart.

6   When Group A are in position, Group B check and if necessary correct Group A.

7   Take away the texts from Group B, giving each student a slip of paper with the name of an instrument. They go and stand with other A and B students in the correct section. They then tell each other as much as they can about their section or instrument.

8   Give the class a gapped version of the original text. Put the students into threes (one A and two Bs) who work together to fill in the blanks and check their information.

9   Finally, the students copy and fill in the blank orchestra chart.

Comments

The first time you use this activity it will need some time to prepare, but you will be able to use it with many different classes.

Acknowledgements

Information taken from www.thinkquest.org/library.

1.10 Correct me

Aims LANGUAGE Drawing conclusions (see Appendix 2); predicting (see Appendix 2).

OTHER Sequencing a text; learning a sequence; reading aloud to correct the teacher; understanding instruction; sharpening observation skills.

Materials A thermometer; a lidded jar big enough to hold the thermometer; a small piece of steel wool; vinegar.

Demo subject CHEMISTRY

TOPIC An experiment demonstrating a chemical reaction

Alternative subjects HISTORY Sequencing events

FOOD TECHNOLOGY Sequencing a simple recipe

DESIGN AND TECHNOLOGY Making an origami figure

Preparation

1   Find a set of instructions and re-write them in a jumbled order.

2   Photocopy one set for each student.

Example Describing an experiment

- Remove the thermometer from the jar.
- Now look at the temperature.
- Wait five minutes
- Write down the temperature.
- Put the thermometer in the jar and close the lid

- Wait five minutes.
- Soak a piece of steel wool in vinegar for one minute.
- Squeeze the vinegar out of the steel wool pad. Wrap the steel wool around the bulb of the thermometer
- Place the thermometer and steel wool back into the jar and close the lid.

Procedure

1 Write a sentence on the board introducing the topic, but leaving a gap for the missing topic word or words. Ask the class to guess the words, in this example, *chemical reaction*.

Example   *A _____ _____ is when elements or compounds interact to form new elements or compounds.*

2 Tell the class you are going to demonstrate the stages of an experiment absolutely silently. The only words they will hear will be: *Wait five minutes.* Tell them to watch very carefully.

3 Demonstrate the experiment silently in slow, clear stages, except for stages two and eight, which you must say out loud.

Example   The following is the correct order:
   i   Put the thermometer in the jar and close the lid.
   ii   Wait 5 minutes.
   iii   Write down the temperature.
   iv   Remove the thermometer from the jar.
   v   Soak a piece of steel wool in vinegar for one minute.
   vi   Squeeze the vinegar out of the steel wool pad. Wrap the steel wool around the bulb of the thermometer.
   vii   Place the thermometer and steel wool back in the jar and close the lid.
   viii   Wait 5 minutes.
   ix   Now look at the temperature.

4 Next give out a photocopy of the experiment stages, telling the students that they are in the wrong order. Ask the students to reorder them correctly based on their memory of your demonstration. They write the numbers 1–9 by the appropriate stage.

5 Read out the jumbled list stage by stage telling the students to correct you by reading out the correct instruction.

6 Ask them what they think will happen to the temperature at the end of the experiment. (It rises because the vinegar removes any protective coating from the steel wool, allowing the steel to rust. When this happens, heat energy is released.) Ask them to guess by how much it will rise.

7 If you are working in the laboratory, get the students to work in small groups to do the experiment, following the correctly ordered instructions. Tell them to check the temperature on the thermometer before they begin. They can check the accuracy of their guesses by seeing how much the temperature has risen at the end of the experiment.

Acknowledgements

This activity was contributed by Simon Marshall. The text was adapted from www.spartechsoftware.com/reeko.

1.11 Parroting

Aims LANGUAGE Learning definitions (see Appendix 2).

OTHER Pronunciation; reading and repeating statements; memorizing important concepts.

Demo subject ICT

TOPIC Computing terms

Alternative subjects LITERATURE Learning a poem or quotes.

HISTORY Learning the dates of important events

MATHEMATICS Learning theorems or formulae

Any subject in which students need to learn information by heart

Preparation

1 Find or write a short text or series of definitions that are important for your students to memorize.

Example

Data	Factual information used as a basis for reasoning, discussion, or calculation.
Digital	A method of encoding information using a binary code of 0s and 1s.
Hardware	Machinery and equipment such as the monitor, the mouse, and the processor.
ICT system	A set up consisting of hardware, software, data, and the people who use them.
Scanner	A device that reads a printed page and converts it into a graphics image for the computer.
Software	Instructions for a computer. Software tells the hardware what to do.

Procedure

1 Write the definitions on the board, leaving a space above each one to add the key words.

2 Dictate the key words. Invite students to come to the board and write the matching key word above each definition.

3 Go through each definition, making sure the students understand them. If necessary translate them into the mother tongue.

4 Read each English definition out loud. Ask the students to repeat after you to focus on the pronunciation.

5 Rub out a part of any sentence, but not any of the key words. Then get the students to read **all** the sentences again, including the part you rubbed out.

Example _____ and converts it into a graphics image for the computer.

6 Rub out a part of another sentence and repeat step 5.

Example A set-up consisting of hardware, software, _____.

7 Continue until all the sentences have disappeared and only the key words are left.

8 Get the students to write the sentences from memory in their books.

Comments

If there are key words, as in this example, it is better to leave them on the board. If there are no key words it seems to help if there are dashes to indicate each line.

1.12 Echoing

Aims	LANGUAGE	Simple past tense.
	OTHER	Listening and repeating; writing; working in groups.
Demo subject	HISTORY	
Topic	Lenin	
Alternative subjects	BIOLOGY	Transpiration of plants
	GEOGRAPHY	Earthquakes
	ART	The Impressionist movement

Any topic your students need to learn and memorize

Preparation

1 Find information in English on the topic and prepare a short talk on it.

2 Divide your input into separate short sentences.

Procedure

1 Write the title of your topic on the board.

Example Vladimir Ilyich Lenin

2 Put the class into groups of not more than four. Ask them to tell each other what they already know about the topic.

3 Write on the board and explain any key words or phrases from your sentences that your students may find difficult to understand.

4 Tell the students to put away their pens and not to use them until you tell them.

5 Ask the members of each group to number themselves one to four.

6   Tell them you are going to read some sentences out loud. You will repeat each one. Every time you stop speaking, one student in each group has to echo to their group exactly what you said. The first time this will be student 1, then student 2 and so on. The whole group then repeats what the 'echoer' said. Alternatively, in a mixed-ability class the echoer could be the highest level student.

7   Read the first sentence twice clearly. The students 1 in each group repeat it, all at the same time. Then the rest of their group repeat it, all together, back to the 'echoer'.

8   Read the second sentence twice for the students 2 to repeat. The groups then repeat it back. Continue in the same way until you have read all the sentences.

Example   i   Lenin was born in 1870 in Russia.
ii   He studied law at university.
iii   He became a professional revolutionary.
iv   He was arrested and exiled to Siberia.
v   After his exile he became the leader of the Bolsheviks.
vi   In 1917 he organized the Bolshevik take-over of power in Russia.
vii   This led to three years of civil war.
viii There was widespread famine.
ix   He died in 1924.
x   His body is in a mausoleum on Moscow's Red Square.

8   Write a key word or two from each sentence on the board.

Example   *born 1870, law university, revolutionary, arrested exiled, after exile, leader Bolsheviks, 1917 organized takeover, power, three years, civil war, famine, 1924, body mausoleum*

9   Tell the students to look at the key words on the board while you re-read all the sentences.

10   Ask the students to reconstruct the sentences in their groups.

11   Check their work.

1.13 ABC dictation

Aims   LANGUAGE   Numbers.

OTHER   Reading; re-ordering sentences; cooperative learning; writing and spelling from listening to a text.

Materials   One piece of paper, preferably A4, per student.

Demo subject   PHYSICS

TOPIC   Space travel

Alternative subjects   FOOD TECHNOLOGY   Bacteria in food

PHYSICS   The principles of pressure

HISTORY   Life story of a historical character

Preparation

1   Choose a text.

2   Divide the text up into twelve short sentences or phrases which would be easy for your students to listen to and write down. Label them A 1–4, B 1–4, C1–4 but in random order. In this example the A students have the shortest sentences and the C students the longest, making it suitable for mixed levels.

Example   **Voyager 1**

A3   Voyager 1 is a spacecraft.

C4   It has travelled 12 billion km to the edge of our solar system.

A1   This long trip has taken 30 years

B3   even though it travels at 35000 mph.

C2   It will take a further 20000 years to reach the Oort Cloud.

C1   This cloud consists of comets that surround our solar system.

B1   Our nearest star is twice as far away as the Oort Cloud.

A2   It is called Proxima Centauri.

B4   We will need new modes of space travel to reach this star.

C3   There are a number of possibilities but none has been tried as yet.

A4   One idea is to use nuclear power.

B2   However, this is very controversial.

Procedure

1   Divide the class into 3 groups, A, B and C.

2   Give each student a piece of paper. Ask them to cut or tear it horizontally into four strips.

3   Tell the class you are going to give them a dictation with a difference. They only write down the information if you say their letter, and each time they write they use a different slip of paper. In this way they will be writing four sentences each. Tell them not to panic if they can't do it the first time as they will have an opportunity to get help later.

4   Write the title of the text on the board, in this example, 'Voyager 1'. If there are any proper names in the text write these on the board also, in this example, *Oort Cloud* and *Proxima Centauri*. Write up and explain any other words you think may be unfamiliar.

5   Read out the sentences at a reasonable speed. Don't pause between them. Start with A1, followed by B1 and C1, then A2 and so on.

6   Put the students into same letter groups and ask them to choose a messenger. In larger classes there can be a number of smaller groups sharing the same letter. They check their sentences and send their messenger to you if they have any gaps or differences. They must all end up with exactly the same sentences. When they have finished checking, you check one set of papers for each group and that student tells their group any corrections you have made.

7   Put students into groups with at least one A, one B and one C in each. If there is more than one student of the same letter, they need to use only one of their sets of papers. Suggest they choose the set that is easiest to read.

8   As a group they put their slips of paper into the right order. They probably won't have realised that you read the text in jumbled order!

9   Read out the text, this time in the correct order, for the class to check. Alternatively, give everyone a copy of the original.

Variation 1

You can make the activity easier by having four groups, A, B, C, D.

Variation 2

It can also be done as a student–student dictation.

1   Dictate the sentences in the correct order, with A1 as the first sentence, B1 the second and so on.

2   Put the chart overleaf on the board for the students to copy.

3   The students write their sentences next to their own letter and leave gaps to fill in the other letters later.

4   Then in ABC groups they dictate their sentences to each other. This is a useful way of avoiding the photocopier, and of getting your students to 'work for' the input.

Acknowledgements

Information taken from www.bbc.co.uk/science/space.

A B C	
A B C	
A B C	
A B C	

1.14 Mutual dictation

Aims LANGUAGE Pronunciation.

OTHER Speaking; listening, reading; writing.

Materials Photocopies of the worksheets.

Demo subject FOOD TECHNOLOGY

TOPIC Bacteria

Alternative subjects ART Using watercolours

PHYSICS Colour

MATHEMATICS Instructions for solving equations

Preparation

1 Write or find a text which gives the students key information.

2 Divide it up into alternate A and B sentences. On one sheet write the A sentences, leaving the B lines blank. Do the reverse on the other sheet.

3 Photocopy the sheets so that you have one A and one B sheet per pair of students.

Student A

Bacteria

A Bugs and germs are the common name for organisms that cause food poisoning.

B _____

A We can only see them through a microscope

B _____

A They can get into our food at any point in the food chain.

B _____

A Food poisoning bacteria multiply fast if they have moisture, food, warmth and time.

B _____

A They are very hard to detect

B _____

Student B

Bacteria

A _____
B They could be bacteria and viruses.

A _____
B so they are also called microbes or micro-organisms.

A _____
B If they are allowed to survive and multiply they can cause illness when that food is eaten.

A _____
B They multiply best between 5 and 63 degrees C.

A _____
B because they do not usually affect the taste, appearance or smell of food.

Procedure

1 Give half the class the A sheets and the other half the B sheets. The easiest way to do this in a larger class is to label alternate rows A and B.

2 Give the students time to read and understand their sentences. They can do this with other students who have the same sheets. If there is anything they don't understand they must ask you. Explain to them that later they may need to explain their sentences to someone else.

3 Write on the board any words you think they may have difficulty pronouncing and work on the pronunciation with them.

4 Put the students into A and B pairs. If you have alternate A and B rows each A can now work with the B student behind them. Tell them not to let their partner see their sheet.

5 Student A starts by dictating their first sentence to Student B. Student B writes it in their first A line. Remind them to dictate the full stops. Student B then dictates their first sentence and Student A writes it in their first B line. They continue like this until they have completed the dictation, and filled in all their lines.

6 They check what they have written by reading it back to each other.

7 Give them time to help each other understand the content.

Comments

Making students work for the information, rather than just giving them a handout, helps them understand and retain it.

Acknowledgements

Information taken from www.howstuffworks.com.

Mutual dictations have been around a long time and we don't know where the idea originated.

1.15 Spot the sentence

Aims LANGUAGE Translating.

OTHER Reading; understanding new information.

Subject Any text your students need to read in a monolingual class.

Preparation

1 Choose any informative text your students need to read in English.

2 Translate the key sentences into the mother tongue.

Procedure

1 Give your students a short time just to skim through the English text.

2 Read out one of the sentences you have translated into the mother

tongue. Ask the class to read out the equivalent English sentence from the text.

3 Continue in this way, reading sometimes a complete sentence, sometimes part of a sentence, sometimes a useful collocation.

4 Put the students into pairs. Looking at the English text, they take it in turns to translate a sentence, part of a sentence or a few words into their mother tongue. Their partner reads out the equivalent English from the text.

Acknowledgements

This is adapted from an activity we learnt from Visnja Anic, first published in *Way To Go Teacher's Book*, Skolska knjiga, Zagreb, 2001.

1.16 What did you hear?

Aims	LANGUAGE	Building vocabulary.
	OTHER	Practising listening skills; predicting.
Demo subject	HISTORY	
	TOPIC	The Wright brothers
Alternative subjects	GEOGRAPHY	Any text concerning constituents of soils
	PHYSICS	Any text explaining electron beams
	ART	Any text on the life and style of a great artist
		Vocabulary for any subject

Preparation

1 Find a text. In the example below the historical information has been simplified and the present tense has been used. Write down key words or dates from the text.

2 Copy the text leaving gaps for the key words or dates. Photocopy the gapped text, one for each student. Keep a copy of the complete text for your own reference.

Procedure

1 Write the title of the text on the board and give the students time to discuss with a partner what they know about the subject.

2 Write the words in bold italics in a column on the board and pre-teach them. (You can write the meanings of these words in the mother tongue.) Get the students to listen and repeat the words. Leave the words on the board, drawing a line to keep them separate.

3 Tell the students that you will read the text twice. They must listen carefully but not take notes. Read the text the first time. After you have done so write the key words in random order on the rest of the board.

4 Read the text again.

The Wright brothers

Every **invention** is very difficult and is the **result** of lots of disappointments and hard work. In the early 20th Century flying is a new idea. It is exciting and dangerous. The American brothers, Orville and Wilbur Wright, build seven flying machines before they are successful. They **crash** many times. They build and **rebuild** their machines. They study <u>gliders</u> and try to find a way to **control** an aircraft. In 1902 they build a glider with wings and a <u>tail</u> that are **flexible**. The Wright brothers begin to plan a powered machine. They ask engine manufacturers to help with engines and <u>propellers</u>, but they are not successful. In 1903 they <u>design</u> and build their own engines and propellers which are better. In France other inventors are trying to win the race to be the first to fly a powered and controlled flying machine. On October 5, 1905 <u>Wilbur</u> Wright makes the first controlled flight. He flies for <u>39</u> minutes and goes <u>24</u> miles (38.6 km) in his Flyer 3. The Wright brothers win the race. The aeroplane is invented.

Example In this text the <u>underlined</u> words would be the gaps. The words in **bold** are the words to pre-teach before reading.

5 Give out the gapped texts. Set a time limit depending on the ability of the class. The students work individually to fill the gaps.

6 Rub out the key words.

7 Now read the text for a third time. Pause at the gaps and ask students to say the missing words.

Follow-up

Ask the students to find out as much as they can about the history of aviation using the Internet, magazines, or textbooks. The information they collect can be used in another lesson for group presentations or exam practice questions.

2
Teaching and activating key vocabulary

Every subject has its own specific key vocabulary. It is often the case that students learning another subject through English do not even know the meanings of these subject words in their mother tongue, which makes the vocabulary learning even more difficult for them. The activities in this chapter are designed both to teach the meanings and to give the students the opportunity to learn and memorize them.

Students need to build a bank of subject-related words and to do this they need training in how to store them on the page, as in 2.7, 'Using mind maps'. A crucial skill is to be able to understand and give definitions and descriptions of words. There are examples of this in 2.1, 'Odd one out', 2.2, 'Right in one' and 2.3, 'Define it'. In addition there are activities focusing on key vocabulary in Chapter 1, where we need to help students understand the vocabulary in a reading or listening text.

Many classroom activities designed to help students learn vocabulary are created by the teacher, but the designing of these activities is in itself a good way to focus on the meaning and use of words. For this reason we have included some student-generated activities such as 2.5, 'Student-generated jumbled words', 2.6, 'Student-generated word puzzles'.

For teachers with monolingual classes there are also some activities such as 2.8, 'Walk and swap' which involve the use of the mother tongue.

2.1 Odd one out

Aims   LANGUAGE Defining and describing (see Appendix 2); spelling.

OTHER   Categorizing words and recognizing word associations; revising specific vocabulary.

Demo subject   BIOLOGY

TOPIC Human biology—parts of the body

Alternative subjects   BUSINESS STUDIES Business terms and abbreviations

PHYSICS Electronic control

HISTORY 20th Century explorers

Preparation

Write lists of related words and add to each list one word which is not related.

Example   A retina, optic nerve, sacculus, iris
B masseter muscle, condyle, radius, temporalis muscle
C scapula, carpals, femur, phalanges, ulna
D fibula, tibia, sternum, patella
E pancreas, coronary artery, left ventricle, pulmonary artery

Procedure

1 Tell the students to write down all the words you dictate. Dictate the first list. Ask the students to work in pairs to check their spelling.

2 Continue in the same way until all the lists have been dictated.

3 Put the students into pairs. Ask them to discuss and underline the 'odd one out' in each of their dictated lists.

4 Ask for a volunteer to write the words from list A on the board. Check the spelling with the class.

5 Call one pair to the board. They underline the 'odd one out' and give a reason for their choice. For example, *The sacculus is the* **odd one out** *because it is in the ear and the others are in the eye.* Check with the other students that they agree.

6 Get another volunteer to write list B and so on, until all the lists are complete and the students have checked their spelling.

7 Clean the board. In pairs, the students test each other on spellings and the meanings.

Answer key

Odd ones out
A sacculus: it is in the ear whereas the others are in the eye.
B radius: it is in the arm whereas the others are in the head.
C femur: this is a leg bone while the others are in the upper body.
D sternum: this is the breastbone; the others are in the leg.
E pancreas: this is the only one not in the heart.

Variation

Give out copies of the lists instead of dictating them.

2.2 Right in one

Aims   LANGUAGE   Question forms (see Appendix 2); modal verbs.

         OTHER   Giving accurate definitions (see Appendix 2); revising key vocabulary.

Materials   Photocopied worksheets; lists of words.

Demo subject   GEOGRAPHY

         TOPIC   Rivers and coasts

Alternative subjects   BUSINESS STUDIES   Finance in business

         PHYSICS   Speed, velocity and acceleration

         BIOLOGY   Diffusion and osmosis

Preparation

1   Write lists of words you want your students to define.

2   Prepare two worksheets, A and B, as in the example below. Prepare the B worksheet in the same way, but with 'Student B' at the head of the top left-hand box. Photocopy the 'Student A' worksheet for half the class and the 'Student B' worksheet for the others.

Example

Worksheet 2.2	
Student A	Right in one
1	1
2	2
3	3
4	4
5	5
My partner's list	Right in one
1	1
2	2
3	3
4	4
5	5

Photocopiable © Oxford University Press

Example   Completed worksheet

Student B	Right in one
1 bay	1 ✗
2 spit	2 ✓
3 wave-cut platform	3 ✓
4 cliff	4 ✓
5 headline	5 ✗
My partner's list	Right in one
1 Meander	1 ✓
2 ox-bow lake	2 ✓
3 levee	3 ✓
4 flood plain	4 ✗
5 alluvium	5 3✓

Procedure

1   Divide the class into two halves, group A and group B. Give out the blank worksheets.

2   Give a list of five words to group A for them to copy down on their prepared worksheet under 'Student A'. Do the same for group B with a different set of words. If the groups are large you may need more than one list of the words for each group.

3   Ask pairs of student As to work together for a few minutes to discuss how they could accurately define their words. Do the same with pairs of student Bs. Give them time to think about the definitions. They do not write anything down.

4   Pair A and B students. Tell them not to show each other their worksheets. Tell them they have to define the words on their list for their partners to guess. They must not say the actual word when they are defining it. The idea is for a pair of students to get as many words 'Right in one' as possible.

5   If the partner guesses correctly at the first try then student A can tick that number in the 'Right in one' box. Student B then writes the word they have defined correctly in 'My partner's list' and ticks the 'Right in one' box. If the guess is not right then Student A must put a cross in the 'Right in one' box.

6   The students could take it in turns to give their definitions.

7   Check which pairs managed to get the most definitions 'Right in one'. At the end of the activity the students check and discuss the definitions which gave them problems. Ask them to write down the problem words and suggest how they could be defined.

2.3 Define it

Aims   LANGUAGE Comparing and contrasting (see Appendix 2); giving definitions (see Appendix 2).

          OTHER   Recalling vocabulary.

Materials Two slips of paper for each student; a small rigid container such as a cardboard or plastic box for each group.

Demo subject BUSINESS STUDIES

          TOPIC Marketing terms

Alternative subjects MUSIC Different kinds of instruments

          DESIGN AND TECHNOLOGY Tools and equipment

          LITERATURE Heroes and creatures in Greek mythology

          Vocabulary for any subject

Procedure

1 Give each student two slips of paper. Put the students into groups of no more than eight. Give each group a container.

2 Write the topic on the board.

Example **Marketing Terms**

3 Explain the rules. This could be done in the mother tongue.

Rules

Each student writes two different expressions to do with the subject, one on each slip. These can be anything to do with the subject. They do not show or tell the other group members what they have written. They fold the slips to hide the writing and put them into the group container. It does not matter if a term is duplicated.

Examples *market research, marketing mix, market share, market penetration, market trend, shrinking market, flat market, niche market, domestic market, segmented market, flooded market, market leader*

4 Choose a student in each group to start the activity. The student takes out one of the slips from the container, reads it silently and gives a definition without using the words written on the slip. If the student does not know the word, they replace it in the container and take another one.

5 The others in the group say what they think it is. They can speak in any order.

6 When a student guesses correctly, he or she keeps the slip, takes another slip from the container, and repeats the activity. If the group fails to guess correctly from the definitions given, the slip is returned to the container for another student to pick out later.

7 Set a time limit depending on the ability of the class. The activity continues until all the definitions have been matched and all the slips removed from the container, or the time limit is reached.

8   When all the slips are out any duplicated items are replaced with different terms. Then the students fold all the slips again and put them back in the container.

9   Repeat the activity but reduce the time limit. This speeding up increases the fun element.

10 The students copy the words and write definitions for homework.

2.4 Two minutes to remember

Aims   LANGUAGE **Defining and describing (see Appendix 2).**

OTHER   **Listening for specific information; note-taking; memorizing key words; learning definitions; visualizing as an aid to revision.**

Demo subject   ENVIRONMENTAL STUDIES

TOPIC **Desert ecosystems**

Alternative subjects   DESIGN ANDTECHNOLOGY **Technical, moral, cultural and environmental values**

ICT **Creating and improving spreadsheets**

PSHE **Developing good relationships and respecting the differences between people**

Preparation

1   Find or write a text that gives key words and examples. The text could be completely new to your students or one they have seen before in their textbook.

2   Make a list of all the key words you will write on the board, and another of the examples you will write around the key words:

Example   Key words: *Location, Climate, Soils, Vegetation, Wildlife, Human activity*

Writing around the key words: *Vegetation—cacti, deep or wide roots, thick bark*

Procedure

1   Write the title of the text on the board. Discuss the title with the students.

2   Write the key words from the text in any order on the board. Draw a box round each key word and leave enough space between the boxes to add the example words given in the text.

Example

| Location | Climate | Soils |
| Human activity | Wildlife | Vegetation |

Example

Desert ecosystems

Deserts are found between 15° and 30° north and south of the equator. The Sahara, in north Africa, is the largest hot desert in the world. Others include the Kalahari in southern Africa, the Atacama in South America, the Gobi in Asia and the Australian Desert.

Deserts have very high temperatures all year. The average daytime temperature is 30° C, but it can reach over 50° C. At night the temperature falls dramatically. It can reach as low as 0°C. Because of the constant high air pressure there is very little rain. On average, deserts get less than 250mm of rain each year.

Desert soils are not very fertile. The soils look grey and are thin with little organic matter. The water evaporates quickly and salt builds up on the soil surface.

However, deserts do have vegetation. The plants adapt to the climate. Some have thick, waxy skins as this helps reduce water loss. Others grow deep, wide roots. The trees protect themselves against fire with thick bark. Cacti can keep water in their fleshy stems.

The deserts also have wildlife. Camels, dingoes, kangaroos, snakes, lizards, spiders and termites are some species that have adapted to the desert environment.

People have managed to live in deserts for many thousands of years. They knew how to survive without damaging the ecosystem. Modern farming practices are changing the desert ecosystems. Overgrazing is causing soil erosion, and the soil is becoming salty as a result of irrigation. Deserts are getting bigger.

3 Tell the students you will read the text twice. Do the first reading. Do **not** discuss the text with the students.

4 Write the example words by the side of the matching key word boxes and draw lines connecting them. Do **not** discuss the examples with the students.

Example

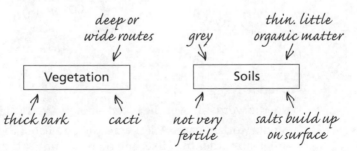

5 Read the text the second time. Tell the students that they have two minutes to memorize the examples.

6 Rub out the examples but leave the key words on the board. Ask the students to work alone, copy the key words and write the examples they can remember. Set a time limit depending on the ability of the class.

7 Students check their work with a partner and add to their list.

8 Call for volunteers to write the examples on the board next to the matching key words. Students copy what is on the board for future reference.

Acknowledgements

Text adapted from *Revise KS3 Geography*, Arnell and Browne, Letts.

2.5 Student-generated jumbled words

Aims   LANGUAGE   Spelling.

      OTHER   Labelling key words on a picture; jumbling and reordering words; using the visual/spatial intelligence.

Materials   Picture to be labelled.

Demo subject   BIOLOGY

      TOPIC   Bones, joints and muscles

Alternative subjects   DESIGN AND TECHNOLOGY   Different equipment/tools

      MATHEMATICS   Geometric shapes

      ART   Pictures and artists

      Vocabulary for any subject

Preparation

1 Find or draw a picture illustrating the words you want to be memorized.

2 Photocopy it for each student.

3 Write a list of the words in random order.

Example   backbone   skull   shoulder blade   ribs   lower arm bones   upper arm bone   collar bones   hand bones

Procedure

1 Write the words all over the board—not in a vertical list.

2 Students work in pairs. Ask them to make a list of the words from the board in any order they like, and then to number them.

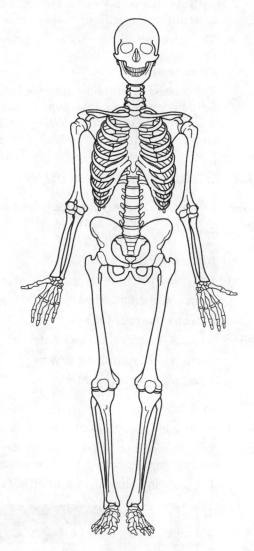

3   Give out the pictures. Now they match the words to their picture by writing the appropriate numbers on the picture. If they have any problems they must get you to check.

4   Get them to jumble the letters of each word on their list.

Example   1   luksl
2   cbakbone
3   laoclr bone
4   lerdoshu blade
5   sbir
6   preup mra bone
7   rwloe mar bones
8   dnah bones

5 Each pair exchanges their picture and their list of jumbled words with another pair. The pairs re-order the letters and then write the matching number from the picture next to each word.

6 They give back their work to the pair who wrote it for them to check.

Comments

The process of jumbling and re-ordering the words is a good way to help students memorize them. In fact they probably learn as much from creating the activity as they do from working on the activity they have been given.

2.6 Student-generated word puzzle

Aims LANGUAGE Writing definitions and descriptions (see Appendix 2); asking and answering questions (see Appendix 2); translating.

Other Memorizing key words.

Demo subject MATHEMATICS

TOPIC Mathematical terms

Alternative subjects BIOLOGY Parts of the body

PHYSICS Electrical components

HISTORY Different battles/wars

Vocabulary for any subject

Preparation

1 Write a list of about twelve words you want your students to focus on.

Example *area, average, coordinates, graph, hypotenuse, numerator, quotient, intersection, integer, equation, denominator, isosceles*

2 Put them in a chart in any order, as below.

#										
1	a	r	e	a						
2	a	v	e	r	a	g	e			
3	c	o	o	r	d	i	n	a	t	e	s
4	g	r	a	p	h						
5	h	y	p	o	t	e	n	u	s	e	
6	n	u	m	e	r	a	t	o	r		
7	q	u	o	t	i	e	n	t			
8	i	n	t	e	r	s	e	c	t	i	o	n
9	i	n	t	e	g	e	r				
10	e	q	u	a	t	i	o	n			
11	d	e	n	o	m	i	n	a	t	o	r
12	i	s	o	s	c	e	l	e	s		

3 Divide the chart in half horizontally across the middle so that the two halves look like this:

Puzzle A

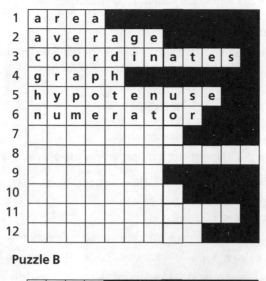

Puzzle B

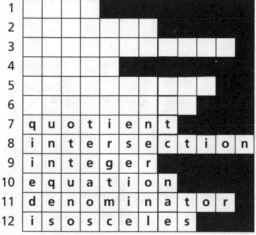

Procedure

1 Put the students into small groups. Give half the groups 'Puzzle A' and the other groups 'Puzzle B'. Ask them in their groups to write a definition or clue for each of the words in their puzzle. These could be done in the mother tongue. Stress that they all need to write the clues, because they will be on their own in the next step.

2 Go round the groups checking their work.

3 Put the students into A and B pairs. Tell them not to let their partner see their chart.

4   Students take it in turns to ask their partner for a clue for any of their blanks, for example, *please give me the clue for number 5*. They write the answers in their chart.

5   Get the students to translate all the words into their mother tongue.

Comments

As with many activities, students probably learn more from writing the clues than from guessing the answers.

2.7   Using mind maps

Aims   LANGUAGE   Categorizing words.

OTHER   Using mind maps; using the visual/spatial intelligence.

Materials   Different coloured pens/crayons.

Demo subject   PHYSICS

TOPIC   Energy

Alternative subjects   SPORT SCIENCE   Different kinds of sport—equipment/venues

GEOGRAPHY   Types of climate—countries/characteristics

BUSINESS STUDIES   Departments—personnel/roles

Vocabulary for any subject

Preparation

1   Prepare a list of words and phrases connected to the topic you want your students to revise.

2   Put them into a mind map. A mind map is a way of organizing and categorizing vocabulary by grouping together words in similar categories. To make a mind map, turn the paper horizontally and write the topic in the middle of the page. In the example on the next page, the topic is 'Energy'. Add a branch from the centre for each key point—preferably using different colours. Then add related vocabulary and concepts to each key-point.

3   Prepare and photocopy a skeleton of the mind map with blanks for the students to fill in.

Procedure

1   Give the students the mind map skeleton with just some of the words filled in.

2   Dictate or write on the board the other words for them to write in the appropriate boxes.

3   Encourage your students to add other words as they arise.

Comments

Encouraging students to make mind maps for different concepts can help them memorize and store new words effectively.

Example

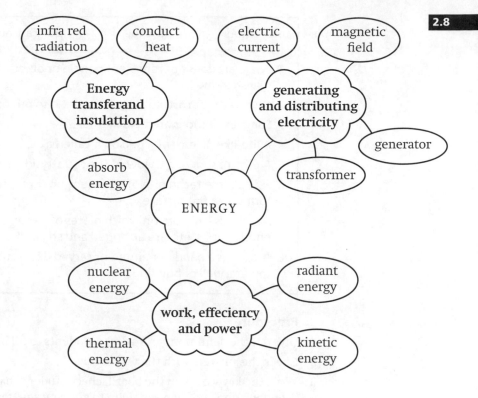

2.8 Walk and swap

Aims   **LANGUAGE** Understanding definitions (see Appendix 2); translating.

         OTHER   Using the kinaesthetic and interpersonal intelligences; cooperative learning; gap-filling.

Materials   One slip of paper per student.

Demo subject   **ART**

Alternative subjects   **BIOLOGY** Parts of a plant

         MATHEMATICS Geometric shapes

         ICT Different input and output devices

         Vocabulary for any subject

Preparation

1 Choose about ten key words you want your students to understand and learn.

2 Write a definition for each leaving a gap for the key word. If you want to make it easier, write the missing key words in a separate box. If you want to make it even easier, give the first letter of each key word. Another variation is to provide the definition in the mother tongue.

3 Photocopy the definitions and the key words so that each student has a copy. Alternatively, write them on the board.

Example

| exhibition | landscape | portrait abstract |
| frieze | gallery | perspective collage |

1 _____ art does not represent people or objects in a realistic way.

2 One way for artists to sell their work is to put on an _____ .

3 Some exhibitions are held in a _____ .

4 A life-like picture of a person is called a _____ .

5 A picture showing a view of the countryside is called a _____ .

6 _____ is the technique of representing three-dimensional forms on a flat surface.

7 A _____ is a picture on which pieces of paper, cloth, photographs, etc. are arranged and stuck.

8 A_____ is a band of painted or carved decoration round the top of a wall or building.

Procedure

1 Give out the definitions and ask the students to fill in the gaps.

2 Check the answers with the whole class.

3 Write the key words on the board, check students have the right pronunciation and then ask them to give you the translation of each key word in their language.

4 Go round the class giving each student a slip of paper and one of the key words.

5 Tell the students they must write the key word you gave them on one side of the paper and the translation in their language on the other side. They must ask you if they need help. Check their translations.

6 Get the students to stand with a partner. Student A of each pair reads out their word in either English or their language, and waits for student B to give them the translation. If student B doesn't know the translation student A tells them and makes them repeat it three times. Then student B reads their word and follows the same process.

7 When they have finished, they exchange papers and go and find another partner. You will need to remind them that they must exchange papers. They repeat the process. Each time they are with a new partner they can choose whether to start with the key word in English or in the mother tongue.

8 Continue like this until they have had a chance to hear most of the words.

9 Ask them to write down from memory all the words they heard plus the translations.

3
Speaking

A common cry from teachers is that they find it hard to get students to speak. They will happily speak about topics unrelated to what we are doing, but getting them to speak about topics of our choice is more difficult. It's very hard to speak in another language about a topic which is unfamiliar. For that reason students need time to prepare and focus on the content before we ask them to speak about it in English. We have included in this chapter some activities, such as 3.6, 'Choose from your list' and 3.7, 'Mini-talks', where students help each other to prepare a speaking activity, so that the planning is done beforehand. In group work in monolingual classes it is often more effective to allow the students to discuss content in the mother tongue before producing the output in English.

Another reason that many students are reluctant to speak in class is shyness and the fear of making mistakes. Many of the activities in this section are done in pairs or in small groups rather than in front of the class. We do not believe that it is always necessary to monitor students' speaking as this can be another deterrent for them. However, many of these activities have a follow-up which may be written and which could be used as evaluation. Examples of small group speaking activities are 3.3, 'Tell me what you know', and 3.7, 'Mini-talks'.

Students get asked a lot of questions but do not often have the chance to practise asking questions. 3.5, 'Right question, right answer', focuses on this. Speaking must involve listening so it is important that the students have specific tasks to carry out when a classmate is speaking, such as note-taking or asking questions. Speaking activities work best when there is a clear tangible outcome because students are then more likely to keep on track, and to see a reason for speaking. Examples of this are 3.1, 'Add to this', and 3.2, 'Ask me, tell me'.

A number of these activities can lead into a writing phase and most of them are a means of helping students to memorize and activate the input they have been given.

3.1 Add to this

Aims   **LANGUAGE**   Linking and sequencing (see Appendix 2); comparing and contrasting (see Appendix 2); pronunciation and intonation practice.

        OTHER   Cooperative learning; working as a group to extend ideas; thinking in more depth about a topic; oral revision.

Demo subject   **GEOGRAPHY**

        TOPIC Australia

Alternative subjects   **ICT** Improving presentation—example of first sentence: *Tables are a good way to present lists*.

        LITERATURE Maya Angelou—example of first sentence: *Maya Angelou was born in 1928 in Missouri*.

        DESIGN AND TECHNOLOGY Systems—example of first sentence: *... consist of separate sections*.

Preparation

Make a list of key facts and features about the topic.

Procedure

1 Write a short, simple sentence about the topic area on the board.

Example **Australia is an island.**

2 Get one student to say it and then ask the class to chorus it.

3 Put the students into groups of four. Tell them you want them to add a word or phrase to the sentence. They can put the words where they like, but the sentence must make sense and still be a complete sentence. As an example you write the second sentence, this helps focus on the topic area:

Example **Australia is an island with deserts.**

The students chorus the example sentence.

4 Give the groups time to discuss and make the sentence longer. Each group writes down their example of a longer sentence. Ask one student from each group to read out their new extended sentence to the class. If the class agree that the new sentences make sense they write them down.

5 As the sentence grows, tell the students that they can take out a word or replace a phrase if this makes it a better sentence. Continue round the groups, adding or replacing words five or six times. Then start again with another topic-linked sentence.

Example **A Australia: facts and features**
- Australia is an island.
- Australia is an island with deserts.
- Australia is an island with 30% desert.
- 30% of Australia is made up of desert.
- Australia has 30% desert and 40% tropics.

- Australia is an island with 30% desert and 40% tropics as well as 30% marginal grazing.
- Australia has 30% desert and 40% tropics as well as 30% marginal grazing.

Example **B The physical features**

- Australia has lots of rivers.
- Australia has lots of rivers, for example, the Darling.
- Australia has lots of rivers, for example, the Darling in the South East.
- There are lots of rivers in Australia, for example, the Darling in the South East and Swan in the South West.

6 At the end of the activity ask the students to write down useful sentences from each topic area. They keep these sentences for revision.

Acknowledgements

Adapted from 'Oral sentence expansion' by Mario Rinvolucri, in *Humanising Your Coursebook*, Delta.

3.2 Ask me, tell me

Aims LANGUAGE Asking for and giving information.

OTHER Note-taking; using fellow students as a resource; cooperative learning; interpersonal skills; revision.

Materials Sheets of paper—one for each student.

Demo subject BIOLOGY

TOPIC Humans as organisms, for example, the digestive system, circulation, the breathing system, respiration, nervous system, the eye.

Alternative subjects PHYSICS Atoms and nuclei

DESIGN AND TECHNOLOGY Plastics and composite material

GEOGRAPHY Coastal management

Any subject you want your students to revise orally

Preparation

Select the topics or units you want the students to revise.
Make a list of useful page references and resource points.

Procedure

1 Give each student a sheet of paper and tell them to fold it in half horizontally. Get them to write the words 'Ask me about' as a title for the top half, and 'Tell me about' as a title for the bottom half.

2 Write your list of topics on the board. Tell the students they must choose one topic they feel confident about and one they feel less confident about. They write the first topic under the heading 'Ask me about', and the second one under the heading 'Tell me about'.

Example

Ask me about

The make-up and functions of blood.

Tell me about

The human digestive system

3 Give the students time to check their information on the 'Ask me about' topic. They can make brief notes in the 'Ask me about' section on their paper.

4 The students now mix and mingle giving their information about their 'Ask me about' topic and collecting information for their 'Tell me about' topic. They write notes in the 'Tell me about' section if they consider the information is correct and helpful. Explain that they should speak to as many people as possible in the time.

5 Write your list of useful references and sources on the board under the appropriate topic titles. At the end of the time limit ask the students to check their information with the references on the board. They should ask you to clarify and correct any information they are not sure about.

6 Ask for volunteers to read out all the correct information they collected for their 'Tell me about' topics. Check that all the topics have been covered. The students listen and make notes about all the topics. They also write down the reference points from the board.

Follow-up

1 The students can turn their papers over and reverse the topics, so the 'Ask me about' topic becomes 'Tell me about' and vice versa. Get the students to repeat the speaking activity but without cues, prompts or note taking.

2 As homework the students can write a few sentences about each topic.

3.3 Tell me what you know

Aims LANGUAGE Asking and answering questions (see Appendix 2).

OTHER Using questionnaires; oral revision; interviewing skills.

Demo subject HISTORY

TOPIC Revision of studied period, for example, the 1960s

Alternative subjects PHYSICS Waves

GEOGRAPHY Climate

BIOLOGY Photosynthesis and the nutrition of green plants

Any subject area

Preparation

Write a worksheet and make copies, one for each student (see the example on the next page). Write an answer key.

Procedure

1 Give each student a copy of the worksheet. Set a time limit. Ask the students to walk round the class and interview as many other students as possible. Tell them to try to find answers for at least eight of the questions before you stop them.

2 On the dotted lines the students make notes of the answers they get and the names of the students who gave them.

3 When they have finished choose a student to read out the information they collected for question 1. Choose a different student to answer for question 2. Continue through the worksheet. Tell the students to keep the questionnaire for future reference.

Follow-up 1

In a later lesson read the questions again and get the students to write down answers individually.

Follow-up 2

Students could work in groups to make their own 'Find someone who…' sheets to be used in the class.

Follow-up 3

Students work in groups and choose one of the questions to turn into a five-minute presentation.

Example

Worksheet 3.3

Find someone who...

1 can name the year President J. F. Kennedy was killed.

_____

2 can give you the names of two US Civil Rights leaders in the 1960s

_____

3 knows which European country the Soviet Union invaded in the late 1960s

_____

4 knows what medical 'first', Christian N. Barnard achieved in 1967

_____

5 can tell you which countries fought in the Six Day War

_____

6 knows when the Berlin Wall was built and demolished

_____

7 knows the names of the first moon walkers and the name of their spacecraft

_____

8 can name a famous sportsperson of the 1960s

_____

9 can name some famous musicians, artists and writers of the 1960s

_____

10 can name a fashion designer and describe the kinds of clothes worn in the 1960s

_____

Answers to questions 1–8

1 1963

2 Martin Luther King and Reverend Abernathy

3 Czechoslovakia

4 heart transplant

5 Israel and Palestine

6 1961 and 1989

7 Neil Armstrong and Buzz Aldrin in Apollo 11

Questions 8, 9, and 10 have numerous answers

3.4 Hear and say

Aims	LANGUAGE	Pronouncing the English alphabet; numbers.
	OTHER	Revising important facts or concepts; memorizing; listening and speaking.
Materials		A set of 'Hear and say' cards for each group.
Demo subject	CHEMISTRY	
	TOPIC	The Periodic Table
Alternative subjects	HISTORY	Dates and battles, reigns, etc.
	LITERATURE	Authors and books
	BIOLOGY	Parts of the body and bones
		Any subjects which involve the use of numbers

Preparation

In this activity each student has a card with two columns, one headed 'Hear' and the other 'Say'. The idea is that when a student hears something that is in their 'Hear' column, he or she responds by saying the item that is directly opposite in their own 'Say' column. This example assumes that there are five students in each group, so you will need five cards per group (see below).

1 Make a set of 'Hear and Say' cards for each group. The easiest way to prepare them is on a computer, but it can also be done on sheets of paper.

2 On each card have two columns headed 'Hear' and 'Say'.

3 Start by writing the name of an element in the 'Say' column on one of the cards, on any line. It's important **not** to start from the top of the card. Underline this word to show that this person is the first to speak. (In this example the student who starts has card 4 with the word 'aluminium' underlined.)

4 Every time you write a word in the 'Say' column you must repeat it on another card in the 'Hear' column. (In this example it is repeated on card 1. The student has to say the letters of the corresponding symbol in the 'Say' column—in this example, Al.)

5 This symbol now has to be written on another card in the 'Hear' column. (In this example it is on card 5. The student who hears it says the word which is opposite in the 'Say' column, i.e. *magnesium*.)

6 This word is repeated on another card in the 'Hear' column. (In this case, card 3.) The student who hears it says the letters of the symbol directly opposite—*Mg*.

7 Continue in this way until the cards are complete. When you finish, write *End* in the 'Say' column, as below on card 1.

8 At this point you will have five 'Hear and say' cards on one sheet of paper. Make a copy for each group of students, i.e. for a class of thirty you will need six copies. Stick each page onto different-coloured paper or card **before** cutting up the cards.

Hear	Say
iodine	I
Mg	nitrogen
Pt	silver
Nb	lithium
aluminium	Al
sodium	END

Hear	Say
B	niobium
nitrogen	N
platinum	Pt
As	iodine
Ca	sodium
I	oxygen

Hear	Say
oxygen	O
Ag	lead
magnesium	Mg
lithium	Li
calcium	Ca
K	arsenic

Hear	Say
borum	B
	aluminium
silver	Ag
arsenic	As
Pb	calcium
N	potassium

Hear	Say
potassium	K
Li	platinum
O	borum
niobium	Nb
lead	Pb
Al	magnesium

Photocopiable © Oxford University Press

Procedure

1 Put the students into groups of five. If there are six in a group two students can share a card. If there are only four, one person has to have two cards. Give each group a set of the cards to share out.

2 Write on the board any words you think your students may have a problem pronouncing. Go through them and check their pronunciation.

3 This is a complicated activity to explain so you might prefer to explain it in the mother tongue, and demonstrate it. Write 'Hear' and 'Say' on the board and tell the class that the words in the 'Hear' column are words that they hear. When they hear one of words in their 'Hear' column, then they must say the word or symbol next to it in their 'Say' column.

4 Ask the students to look for a word which is underlined in their 'Say' column. If they see one, they raise their hands. Get them to say the word to their group.

5 Ask the students with that word in their 'Hear' column to raise their hands. Tell them to say the word or symbol that is directly opposite.

6 Continue like this until your students know what to do.

7 If you want your students to repeat the activity, they should first exchange cards within their groups, so as to practise a different set of elements and symbols.

Comments

This is a complicated activity which needs some preparation, but it is well worth the effort. If you have it on cards you can use it again and again. Students love it, and it has the advantage of making them speak and listen, as well as reading. It's the kind of activity that you can bring out as a revision or filler at any time.

Variation

Get groups of students to make their own 'Hear and say' cards on a specific topic.

Acknowledgements

The process of 'Hear and say' cards has been around a long time. We do not know where it originated.

3.5 Right question, right answer

Aims	LANGUAGE	Formulating precise questions (see Appendix 2); defining (see Appendix 2); comparing and contrasting (see Appendix 2).
	OTHER	Revising key words; learning definitions.
Materials		Copies of Worksheet 3.5, adapted for your subject.
Demo subject	BUSINESS STUDIES	
	TOPIC	Business terms and abbreviations
Alternative subjects	SCIENCE	Equipment and experiment processes
	HISTORY	Any important dates, treaties and people
	MATHS	Formulae, signs and symbols
		Vocabulary for any subject

Preparation

1 Write lists of the words/expressions/terms/abbreviations you want your students to revise.

2 Prepare A and B worksheets. Photocopy A for half the class and B for the other half. You could make the activity more demanding by making three different sets, A and B, C and D, E and F, with different words. This reduces the problem of students hearing others asking similar questions.

Procedure

1 Put the students into pairs. Give out the worksheets.

2 Read the general instruction at the top of the worksheet to the class and check that students understand what they have to do.

Example

Student

Instructions

Your partner is going to ask you some questions. They have five minutes to ask you their questions.

- After five minutes it is your turn to ask your partner questions. There are ten words, expressions, or abbreviations below. Ask your partner questions so that they will answer with the exact words you have on your sheet.
- For example, if the word is FACTORY you could ask *What is the general name we call a place where a product is made?*
- You have only five minutes for all ten questions, so go on to another question if you are having problems. You can come back to this question later. Tick (✓) the 'Yes' box every time your partner answers with the correct word.
- When you have finished, tick the 'No' boxes for any answers your partner failed to get. Work together with your partner and try to suggest better questions to get these answers.

	Yes	No
1		
2		
3		
4		
5		
6		
7		
8		
9		
10		

Photocopiable © Oxford University Press

3   Tell the students that you will time them for five minutes and when you call *time out*, student B must stop. You will then start timing another five minutes for student A to ask questions. At the end of the second five minutes the questioning must stop. Alternatively the pairs can time themselves.

4   At the end of the activity check which questions gave correct answers and which failed to do so, and discuss them. Also check the words, expressions and abbreviations. The students make notes.

Worksheet 3.5a
Student A

Instructions

1 Your partner is going to ask you some questions. They have five minutes to ask you their questions.

2 After five minutes it is your turn to ask your partner questions. There are ten words, expressions or abbreviations below.

3 Ask your partner questions so that they will answer with the exact words you have on your sheet. For example, if the word is FACTORY you could ask—*What is the general name we call a place where a product is made?*

4 You must not mention the word.

5 You have only five minutes for all ten questions, so go on to another question if you are having problems. You can come back to this question later.

6 Tick (✓) the 'Yes' box every time your partner answers with the correct word.

7 When you have finished, tick the 'No' boxes for any answers your partner failed to get.

8 At the end work together with your partner and try to suggest better questions to get these answers.

	Yes	No
1 e-commerce		
2 merger		
3 CEO		
4 logo		
5 headhunter		
6 brand loyalty		
7 Virgin		
8 target consumer		
9 KPI		
10 plc		

Worksheet 3.5b
Student B

Instructions

1 Your partner is going to ask you some questions. They have five minutes to ask you their questions.

2 After five minutes it is your turn to ask your partner questions. There are ten words, expressions or abbreviations below.

3 Ask your partner questions so that they will answer with the exact words you have on your sheet. For example, if the word is FACTORY you could ask—*What is the general name we call a place where a product is made?*

4 You must not mention the word.

5 You have only five minutes for all ten questions, so go on to another question if you are having problems. You can come back to this question later.

6 Tick (✓) the 'Yes' box every time your partner answers with the correct word.

7 When you have finished, tick the 'No' boxes for any answers your partner failed to get.

8 At the end work together with your partner and try to suggest better questions to get these answers.

	Yes	No
1 competitor		
2 company report		
3 benchmarking		
4 joint venture		
5 targets		
6 cash flow statement		
7 marketing mix		
8 Sony		
9 slogan		
10 USPs		

Abbreviations

CEO Chief Executive Officer
KPI Key Performance Indicators/Key Product Indicators
plc Public Limited Company
USP Unique Selling Point

Variation 1

Make worksheets with some gaps. The students work in pairs to add their own words, expressions, abbreviations, dates or figures before they start asking the questions.

Follow-up

Use the information for planning revision and future lessons.

Acknowledgements

This activity and the worksheets are adapted from *Pair Work 2*, Peter Watcyn Jones, Penguin.

3.6 Choose from your list

Aims LANGUAGE Preparing and giving a short talk on a specific subject; memorizing words.

OTHER Making revision lists; note-taking; listening.

Materials Screen or poster for display

Demo subject BIOLOGY

TOPIC Animal and plant cells

Alternative subjects HISTORY Important events in a particular period; famous people in a particular period

MUSIC Mozart operas

SPORTS SCIENCE/PHYSICAL EDUCATION Different training methods

Any topic which can generate a list

Preparation

Display these instructions or make copies for the students.

---

1 Write notes in your language on the content you want to include.

2 In your head, give your talk using your language.

3 Re-write your notes in English. Don't write full sentences. Ask me for help or use your dictionary.

4 In your head, give your talk in English. Make a note of any language you still need help with, and ask me or use your dictionary.

5 Repeat your talk once more in English in your head.

Procedure

1 Ask the students to write a list of words on a given topic. Tell them that if they don't know the words in English they can write them in their mother tongue to start with.

Example *Animal and plant cells nucleus, cytoplasm, cell membrane, mitochondria, vacuole, chloroplast, cell wall*

2 Students translate into English any words they wrote in the mother tongue. They do this with the help of their partner, a dictionary, their coursebook or you.

3 Tell the class that they are going to give a short description (not more than 3 minutes) of one item that they choose from their list.

4 Show the instructions on a screen or give each student a photocopy of them.

5 Give the students time in class to prepare, or ask them to do this for homework, using their dictionaries. They can check any questions with you in the next lesson.

6 Put the students into pairs or small groups. They take it in turns to give their talks, while the listeners take notes.

Follow-up 1

Students write about their chosen topic.

Follow-up 2

Students describe someone else's topic to a student from a different group.

Follow-up 3

Students describe their topic to the class and the class have to guess the original word.

3.7 Mini-talks

Aims LANGUAGE Writing questions (see Appendix 2).

OTHER Preparing and giving a short talk; recalling previously taught topics; giving concise information; listening; cooperative learning.

Materials One piece of paper per group.

Demo subject HISTORY

Alternative subjects BIOLOGY The nervous system; blood

MATHEMATICS Perimeter, area, volume; probability

LITERATURE Shakespeare; Dante

Any other subject your students have been learning about

Preparation

Decide on two topics you want your students to talk about.

Example   World War 1
Russia and the USSR

Procedure

1 Put the students into groups of four to six, so that you have an equal number of groups. Pair off the groups. Give each pair of groups one of the topics.

2 Ask each group to choose a specific aspect of the topic for each person in their pair-group to talk about for up to three minutes. This could take the form of a statement or a question. They should write these, followed by the names of the students in the other group, on a sheet of paper.

Example   **World War 1**

   a *How did the peace treaties of WW1 change the map of Europe?*
   Name of person to talk about it.

   b *Which different countries were involved in the war?*
   Name of person to talk about it.

   c *Describe the trenches*
   Name of person to talk about it.

   d *Name and describe an important figure in WW1*
   Name of person to talk about it.

3 The groups exchange their papers. Give everyone time to make notes about their topic.

4 In their groups each person talks in the mother tongue about their topic. The group discuss each topic, adding or changing anything they think necessary. They can ask you for help.

5 Give everyone time to practise saying their topic to themselves, but this time in English. They may prefer to do this walking around.

6 Students now take it in turns to give their talk in English to their own group. The group can offer help if needed.

7 Put the pair-groups together. Each person gives their prepared talk in English.

Follow-up

1 For homework they could write up their talks.

2 Each group could give a joint presentation as a project product.

4

Writing

There are many activities in this book which include a writing component, but this chapter focuses on practising some basic writing skills. The tasks range from writing a few sentences to writing a longer text. Writing about complex topics in another language is a demanding task. For that reason we have included in this chapter some activities which focus on the basics of writing such as spelling—see 4.1, 'How do you spell it?', and 4.2, 'Spelling practice'.

Arming students with the chunks of language they will need to express different concepts and functions, for example, defining and comparing, is another important area and the activity 4.3, 'Mixed language functions', gives ideas on how to work on this. A further important writing skill is summarizing. Many students take information from a book or the Internet and then just copy and paste it rather than summarising or re-writing it in their own words. 4.5, 'Summarizing', 4.6, 'Elastic sentences', 4.7, 'Exactly 50 words' and 4.8, 'It pays to advertise', focus on this skill.

Because writing can be a lonely, rather daunting, experience we have suggested doing some of these writing tasks with a partner or in a group. An obvious alternative is to set them as homework, but in this case it would sometimes be helpful to allow students to work together in the planning stages in class. Finally, students need to learn to edit their own writing and 4.4, 'Self-editing', gives a way of encouraging them to do this.

4.1 How do you spell it?

Aims	LANGUAGE Practising difficult spellings; the sounds of the alphabet; pronunciation.
Materials	Sets of worksheets.
Demo subject	MATHEMATICS
Alternative subjects	BIOLOGY Parts of a plant
	DESIGN AND TECHNOLOGY Different materials
	MUSIC Names of composers
	Any topics which contain difficult spellings

Preparation

Prepare two worksheets (see example below) and photocopy enough for half the class to have Worksheet 4.1a and the other half to have Worksheet 4.1b.

Example

Worksheet 4.1a	Worksheet 4.1b
Say	Say
1 quadrilateral	1 horizontal
2 circumference	2 isosceles
3 symmetrical	3 perpendicular
4 perimeter	4 parallelogram
5 approximately	5 coordinate
6 rectangle	6 square

Write B's words	Write A's words
1	1
2	2
3	3
4	4
5	5
6	6

Write your words	Write your words
1	1
2	2
3	3
4	4
5	5
6	6

Photocopiable © Oxford University Press

Procedure

1 Read out the words from your list and ask the students to repeat them so as to focus on the pronunciation. Also check that they remember the meanings.

2 Put the students into pairs, A and B. Give them the worksheets. Make sure they don't see each other's words.

3 Write these instructions on the board:
   - *A says a word from the 'Write B's words' column*
   - *B writes it down in the 'Write Your Words' column*
   - *B spells the word back aloud.*
   - *A checks it.*
   - *Repeat this process with B saying a word from the 'Write A's words' column.*

4 Student A starts by spelling out the first word in their 'Say' column while student B writes it in the 'Write A's words' column. Student B then says the word out loud. Next student B spells the first word in their 'Say' column while A writes it in the 'Write B's words' column. Student A then says the word out loud. They continue like this until they have spelt out all their words.

5 When they have finished they check their spellings with each other.

6 Next they must fold their worksheets so that they cannot see the 'Say' column.

7 They now take it in turns to say, but not spell out, the words they wrote in their first 'Write' column while their partner writes them in their 'Write your words' column.

8 They check their spellings with their partners.

4.2 Spelling practice

Aims LANGUAGE Working on difficult spellings; saying and understanding the letters of the alphabet.

OTHER Repetition; memorizing; using the kinaesthetic intelligence.

Demo subject ENVIRONMENTAL STUDIES

Alternative subjects CHEMISTRY Different elements

MUSIC Different composers

GEOGRAPHY Different eco-systems

Difficult words to spell in any subject

Preparation

Prepare a list of words your students find difficult to spell.

Example artificial   carnivore   insecticide
dairy   deciduous   pollute
reservoir   deforestation

Procedure

1 Write the words all over the board—not in a vertical list. This is so that the students can pick any words they like in step 3.

2 Put the students into pairs. Tell them they are going to take it in turns to choose a word from the board and to write it with their finger on their partner's back. Their partner has their back to the board.

3 Demonstrate with a student whose back is to the board. Write each letter of the word separately and ask the student to say it out loud, before you continue with the next letter. The student first says the word, then spells it out without looking at the board.

4 Stop the activity when they have all written two words on their partner's back.

5 Tell them they must now choose one other word which they write with their finger on the desk.

6 Finally ask them to choose any remaining words and write them with their finger in the air.

7 Rub the words off the board and ask the students to write them from memory.

Comments

We know that it would not be acceptable to use 'back writing' with all classes, in which case just use the desk and the air-writing suggestions. However, where 'back writing' is acceptable, it is a great way for your students to use their kinaesthetic intelligence to feel the words and get the spellings inside them!

4.3 Mixed language functions

Aims   LANGUAGE **Expressing different language functions.**

Other   **Writing.**

Materials   **Prepared sentences; cards or slips of paper for each student.**

Demo subject   ICT

     TOPIC **Output devices**

Alternative subjects   HISTORY **Different types of government**

     GEOGRAPHY **Natural disasters**

     CHEMISTRY **Acids and alkalis**

     The specific functions needed for any subject

Preparation

1 Analyze your lesson and identify the language functions your students will need to be able to express and understand in English, for example, predicting, classifying, hypothesizing, showing cause and effect, defining, comparing and concluding. There are examples of this language in Appendix 2.

2 Write in English sentences which demonstrate the language functions you want to work on. These could be from the coursebook. Write the name of the function in the students' language. In this example the functions are: *defining/naming, classifying, comparing, consequence, predicting*

Example

Defining/Naming

- An output device is any hardware used to communicate the result of data processing carried out by CPU.
- A bubble–jet printer is an ink-jet printer that works by heating the ink and spraying it on to paper.
- The printhead is the component which sprays jets of ink onto the paper.
- The two main types of monitor are LCDs and CRTs.
- A Visual Display Unit (VDU) is the most commonly used output device.

Classifying

- There are three main types of printer.
- There are three different ways of controlling the flow of ink—by crystals, by heating the ink, or by continuous flow.
- There are two ways that monitors differ from each other – size and resolution.

Comparing

- Ink-jet printers cost less than laser printers.
- Ink-jet printers produce better quality printouts than dot-matrix printers.
- There are many more nozzles on an ink-jet than dots on a dot-matrix.
- An ink-jet printer is slower than a laser printer.

Consequence

- Laser printers contain complex equipment, so they are expensive to repair.
- Laser printers have at least 600 dots per inch (dpi), which means they can print high-quality documents.
- Hydraulic actuators are slow but very powerful, so they are useful for lifting heavy equipment.
- There are many nozzles on an ink-jet so the print resolution is good.

> ### Predicting
>
> - As colour page (laser) printers get cheaper and better there will be less demand for small graph plotters.
> - Voice synthesizers will sound more human in the future.
> - The price of laser printers will come down.

Procedure

1 Write on the board in the mother tongue the names of the language functions you want to work on, and ask the class to give you examples of how to express them in the mother tongue: for example, comparing, predicting, etc.

2 Give the students some examples of how to express these functions in English.

3 There are a number of possible ways of doing the next step.
   - Give the students all the sentences in a jumbled order and ask them to group them according to their language function.
   - Write the names of the language functions in the mother tongue on different cards or slips of paper and distribute them so each student has one. Read out the sentences in jumbled order and ask the students with the matching function to read it out.
   - Give each student one of the sentences in English on a slip of paper. Call out one of the language functions in the mother tongue. The students with the matching English sentences read them out.
   - Give small groups of students the English sentences on separate slips and the names of the five language functions in the mother tongue on different slips. They match them up.

4 Ask students to write another example on the same topic for each language function.

Acknowledgements

Content taken from *GCSE ICT Revision Guide*, Richard Parsons (ed.), Coordination Group Publications Ltd.

4.4 Self-editing

Aims LANGUAGE Checking written work; self-editing; writing.

TOPIC Any subject where students are required to write in English

Preparation

1 Find a text from the book, or write one yourself, and add some language mistakes.

2 Make a copy of the text for each student or put it on a screen. Alternatively, you could use past student work. It is up to you what kind of mistakes to include. This will vary according to the students' mother tongue. In this example there are: missing auxiliary, spelling, word order, word missing, wrong word.

Example

> It's good idea to check your written work before to give it to your teacher. Everybody does mistakes sometimes, even in there own language. It not takes much time to read through and edit carefully. You might like to use a checklist for helping you. Take one item on the checklist at a time and go through your writing to make sure it is OK in that departement. You probably know what kind of mistakes you do, so why you don't write your own checklist? Here is an example of one:
>
> - Have I remembered the -s on the third person singular?
> - Have I got the right word order in the wh-questions?
> - Are all the verbs in the right tense?
> - Have I used the present continuous where it should be the present simple?
> - Have I got the negative sentences right? i.e. don't/doesn't
> - Are there any words missing? For example, the/a/an
> - Have I put the adjectives before the noun?
> - Is the word order OK?

Photocopiable © Oxford University Press

Procedure

1 Brainstorm with the class their most common mistakes. Write them on the board. Go through them and make sure everyone understands and agrees on the correct version of these mistakes.

2 Explain that you are going to give the class a text which contains some mistakes. They should use the list of mistakes on the board as a checklist.

3 Give out the text or show it on a screen.

4 Get each student to write their own personalized checklist following the example.

5 Give them a topic to write about. This could be for homework.

6 When they have finished writing tell them to use their checklist to look for mistakes.

7 Ask them to exchange their writing with a partner. They use their checklist to check for their partner's mistakes.

4.5 Summarizing

Aims LANGUAGE Summarizing; expanding sentences; picking out key information; writing; learning key information.

Demo subject GEOGRAPHY

TOPIC Glaciers

Alternative subjects BIOLOGY Photosynthesis

BUSINESS STUDIES The break-even point

MUSIC Description of jazz

Any topic in which you want your students to focus on succinct information.

Preparation

1 Find two sentences which contain key information.

2 Take out everything but the bare bones from one of the sentences.

Example **Original sentence**

As glaciers move downhill they cause massive erosion of the land, carving out huge U-shaped valleys.

Reduced sentence

Glaciers cause erosion, carving out valleys.

Removed words

as, U-shaped, move downhill, of the land, they, huge, massive

Procedure

1 Put the reduced sentence on the board.

2 Dictate the words you removed. Don't dictate them in the original order. Let the students compare notes and ask you if they have any problems in understanding or spelling the words.

3 Tell the students these words came from the original sentence. Their job is to put them back so as to create the original sentence.

4 When students are ready, dictate the original sentence for them to check their answers. Alternatively, ask a student to write their solution on the board.

5 Write your second complete sentence on the board and ask the students to reduce it to the bare bones.

Example *Corries, which are also known as cirques and cwms, are deep circular hollows near mountain tops where glaciers, up to two km across, are formed.*

Comments

This activity could be followed by the more difficult activity 4.6, 'Elastic sentences'.

4.6 Elastic sentences

Aims **LANGUAGE** Cause and result (see Appendix 2); conjunctions.

OTHER Editing and improving written work; practising writing and spelling.

Materials Sheets of paper for students to write on.

Demo subject **LITERATURE**

Topic Greek mythology

Alternative subjects **GEOGRAPHY** Cities and their problems

HISTORY Inventions in the 19th Century

PHYSICS Electric circuits

Preparation

Write a list of sentence beginnings related to the topic.

Example A *Achilles was killed by Paris when…*
B *Furies were spirits who tormented…*
C *The Elysian Fields were…*
D *Jason and the Argonauts were searching for…*

Procedure

1 Put the students into groups of four. Tell them that you are going to dictate a list of sentence beginnings. When they write these down they should leave a space after each one, so they can write an ending later.

2 Dictate the list. Ask the students to check with their partners for correct spelling. Check with the class and write any problem spellings on the board.

3 Tell the students to work individually and write their own sentence endings.

4 When they have worked through the list the students take it in turn to read their sentence endings to the rest of their group.

5 Each group discusses the sentence endings. Then they put all the information together, extending the original sentence into a short paragraph. One member of the group writes down their final effort.

6 Each group exchanges their written work with another group who check, correct and challenge the writing. You check with them.

7 Display the finished versions.

Comments

Not many students want to spend time improving and editing their work once they have written it. This activity helps them see how useful and satisfying it is to improve draft copies.

4.7 Exactly fifty words

Aims LANGUAGE Writing summaries; reading; writing; taking in important information; skimming and scanning.

Subjects Any reading text

Materials A copy of the chosen text for each student, sheets of paper to write on

Preparation

Choose the text you want your students to understand and remember. Make a note of the key points.

Procedure

1 Give your students the text and ask them to read it through once to get the gist of it. Give them a time limit.

2 Ask them to read it again, but this time to underline the key points. They also need to write on a separate piece of paper any proper names and numbers.

3 Give them a short time to compare and discuss their underlinings with a partner.

4 Ask students to write their names on their texts. Then take them in.

5 Students write a summary of the text using exactly fifty words. This could be done as a homework activity.

6 Give back the original texts.

Comments

This activity is a good way to train your students to research information and then put it into their own words. It helps to discourage the 'cut and paste' approach to the information they find on the internet.

Acknowledgements

This idea was contributed by Katie Plumb.

4.8 It pays to advertise

Aims   LANGUAGE Contrasting and comparing (see Appendix 2).

OTHER   Focusing on key issues; working in groups; using a variety of resources; summarizing; note-taking.

Materials   Overhead projector, electronic whiteboard, or photocopies of texts.

Demo subject   ENVIRONMENTAL STUDIES

TOPIC Environmental flashpoints

Alternative subjects   DESIGN AND TECHNOLOGY Products and quality

HISTORY Great explorers

BUSINESS STUDIES Marketing your product

Preparation

Find a few examples of texts about one of the topics which present information in a variety of ways, and either photocopy them for the students or prepare them for display on a poster, projector, or electronic whiteboard. You can use texts from books, CD-ROMs, or the Internet. By comparing the examples the students will see different ways of presenting information, for example, some have easy-to-follow diagrams, others have the language level simplified, some have graphs and charts. Showing how different text types deal with the same topic helps the students appreciate the importance of researching different areas for information.

Procedure

Lesson 1

1 Show your text examples. Ask your students to explain what makes one text more interesting, informative or reliable to read than another.

2 Put the students into groups of three or four.

3 Write up the list of topics you want your students to research and display.

Example Greenhouse effect, Global warming, Acid rain, Desertification

If you have a large class the topics can be repeated.

4 Negotiate with the groups which topics they will research. Write down the topic and the names of the students in that group. Keep this information for reference.

5 Give the students time to find different texts about their chosen subject from books or the Internet. Each group decides which text to use and copies it. Check that the students give the text reference. This can be done in class time if the material is easily available, or as homework.

6 The students study the text and decide what questions they think the text answers. They write the questions down.

Example **Desertification**

A *What is desertification?*
B *Where are the problem areas?*
C *What problems and hazards does it create?*
D *How can we improve the situation?*

Ask them to write down what extra information the text gives, for example, diagrams, charts, statistics, photographs etc.

Lesson 2

1 Each group writes a short advertisement to 'sell' their article to the other students. Check the written advertisements.

Example If you want to know what desertification is and how it works, then this is the article you should read. It is clear, attractive and easy to follow. It will only take you a few minutes to find the answers to such questions as … (*list the questions*). The text also has colourful and easy-to-follow diagrams/charts/graphs etc.

2 The groups present their texts to the rest of the students who listen and write notes about the different texts and the questions they answer.

3 Students pin up the texts and the advertisements they have written for them. The other students walk round and note down the reference points and their own feelings about the appearance of the texts.

Comments

This activity helps the students to build up a bank of texts. It also encourages them to look at different resource areas. You could repeat the activity during the term to create a reference library of subject texts.

For useful websites see Appendix 4.

4.9 Noughts and crosses

Aims LANGUAGE Discussing and writing definitions (see Appendix 2).

OTHER Summarizing and editing; cooperative learning; revising and writing short definitions of words, phrases, expressions, symbols and signs.

Materials Slips of paper.

Demo subject BUSINESS STUDIES

TOPIC Business abbreviations and terms

Alternative subjects ICT Measurement, control and simulation

PHYSICS Energy

MUSIC Tempo and dynamics (use the bass and treble clef signs instead of noughts and crosses)

Vocabulary for any subject

Preparation

Write a list of items, words, abbreviations, symbols and expressions you want explained. You will need nine items for the beginning of the activity and a few more to hold in reserve.

Procedure

1 Draw a 'noughts and crosses' grid on the board and check that the students understand the rules of the game.

Rules for 'Noughts and Crosses'

One team is represented by noughts '0' and the other by crosses 'X'. The teams take it in turns to write their '0' or 'X' on the grid. The aim of the game is to be the first team to form a line of three, horizontally, vertically or diagonally. With the activity here the students have to answer a question to get their symbol each time and only if they give a correct answer do they get their '0' or 'X' to put into the grid. It is important that the group thinks about the strategy of where they place their '0' or 'X' so that they can win the line.

Photocopiable © Oxford University Press

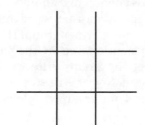

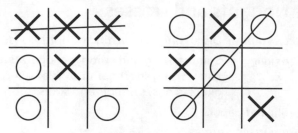

2 Write the words, expressions, or abbreviations you want the students to explain in the noughts and crosses grid on the board. Each student makes a copy of the grid.

Example

outsourcing	HR	assembly line
logisitics	consumer	quality control
MD	depreciation	shareholders

Abbreviations

MD   Managing Director
HR   Human Resources

3 Put the students into an even number of groups. Pair up the groups, calling them groups A and B. Give each group slips of paper. Ask each pair of groups to toss a coin to find which group will be **noughts** and play first, and which group will be **crosses** and play second. Give the groups discussion time before they start the activity.

4 The group that wins the toss chooses one abbreviation and whispers together to agree on an explanation. They write this down on a slip of paper. They pass the slip to their partner group. The partner group can accept or reject the explanation. You are the final judge. If the explanation is accepted then the groups write a nought in the abbreviation box on their grid. Now it is the turn of the **crosses.** They continue the game until one group completes a line and wins.

5 If both groups fail to explain the same grid item, then the teacher replaces that item with one of the extra words from the prepared list and the group who first tried to explain the word has first chance to try again. At the end of the activity check who the winners are. Write any of the abbreviations they found difficult on the board and ask the class to explain. Also explain any unanswered items.

6 Get all the students to copy down the list of items from the grid plus any of the extras that were used. Ask them all to write clear explanations for homework.

4.10 Do you recognize me?

Aims LANGUAGE **The past tense; paraphrasing words (see Appendix 2); defining and comparing (see Appendix 2); drawing conclusions (see Appendix 2).**

OTHER **Learning vocabulary; note-taking.**

Materials **Slips of paper.**

Demo subject HISTORY

TOPIC **Inventions in transport**

Alternative subjects ICT **Data access**

BUSINESS STUDIES **Different job descriptions**

DESIGN AND TECHNOLOGY **Mechanisms to change the direction of motion**

Preparation

Write out the list of words you want defined and the key points you want included in the definitions. You need one word for each pair of students, but if you have a large class the words can be repeated.

Example *helicopter, vertical take-off and landing aeroplane, jets, monorail, sea-plane, hydrofoil, TGV, hovercraft, airships, submarines, barges*

Procedure

Lesson 1

1 Put students into pairs. Give each pair a word from your list.

2 Tell them that each student should write two definitions for their word, one easy and one more difficult. This gives them practice when reading a detailed text or definition and recognizing the key information. It also helps them to write this key information in their own words. It is good practice for note-taking.

Students can do this for homework using their notes, textbooks and the Internet.

Example *Hovercraft—easy definition*
This vehicle floats above roads and water.

Hovercraft—more difficult definition
This type of transport was invented by Christopher Cockerell in the mid 1950s. It uses compressed air to move. It has been used for commercial and military purposes ever since.

Lesson 2

1 Get the students to work in their pairs to check and discuss their definitions. They then agree which two definitions to use. Each pair improves their final definitions and checks with you. You check that your key points have been included.

2 The students write the easy definition on one slip, titled 'Easy', and the more difficult definition on the other slip, marked 'More Difficult'.

3 Each pair joins another pair. They don't show each other the slips of paper. The student with the 'More Difficult' slip reads the definition to the other pair and asks them to guess what word they are defining. After the other pair has guessed, the student with the 'Easy' slip of paper reads that definition to check that the guess is correct. The activity is repeated so that both pairs of students have listened, and guessed the words.

4 The students move on to other pairs and repeat the activity until they have listened and guessed most of the words. Set a time limit for the whole class activity. It doesn't matter if they hear other definitions for their own words.

5 At the end of the time limit the pairs staple their two definition slips together and give them to you.

6 Write the list of words on the board. The students write definitions of the words in their textbooks. Ask for volunteers to read out their definitions.

Lesson 3

For quick revision in a following lesson, you read a selection of the stapled definitions and all the students write down the target words.

4.11 Student–student questions

Aims LANGUAGE Writing questions and answers (see Appendix 2).

OTHER Responding quickly to written questions; revision; exam practice; group discussions.

Materials Lots of slips of paper big enough for a question and an answer.

Demo subject DESIGN AND TECHNOLOGY

TOPIC Packaging

Alternative subjects BIOLOGY Plant senses (responses to light, gravity, water, etc.)

MATHEMATICS Mental arithmetic

ICT Databases

Any subject you want to revise

Procedure

1 Write on the board the topic(s) you want the students to work on.

2 Give the students a short time to look at their notes to remind themselves about the topic(s).

3 Give about four blank slips of paper to each student.

4 Ask each student to write their name on one of the slips of paper. Take in the papers and redistribute them, making sure no one gets their own name.

5 Tell the students they are going to write one question about the given topic on this slip of paper. They must put their name at the end, and then give the slip to the student named on the paper. When they receive an answer they keep the paper to check later. When they receive a question, they answer it on the same slip of paper and return it to the sender.

6 Now they can write another question to anyone they choose, using a different slip of paper. Again, when they receive an answer, they keep the slip of paper to check later.

7 Stop the activity when you think it has gone on long enough. They don't necessarily have to use all four slips of paper.

8 Put the students into groups of about six. They read out their questions and answers and discuss together whether the answers are correct. If they have any doubts they ask you.

9 Get each group to choose the two questions which they think are the most difficult. They read these out to the rest of the class. Give the groups a short time to discuss the answers. Then check the answers with the whole class.

5

Consolidation and revision

The pressure to 'get through' the syllabus is a problem for us all. If we do not allow time for consolidation there is a danger that we 'get through' it but our students do not retain it. Recapping is an important stage of learning for all our learners and crucially it gives the slower learners a second opportunity to understand. This chapter offers different ways to consolidate and revise the input. In addition to recapping, these activities also give our students the opportunity to speak, listen, read, and write in English about the subject, so they serve a dual purpose.

5.3, 'Who or what am I?', and 5.2, 'Jumbled sentences', focus particularly on revising vocabulary. Some of the activities, such as 5.8, 'Definition bingo' and 5.9, 'On target' are more game-based. Others, such as 5.5, 'A word beginning with' and 5.6, 'Call our bluff' are student-generated. Revising for exams can be a lonely and boring process. 5.13, 'Three things I know about' and 5.14, 'Give me four', encourage students to revise together and fill in the gaps in their knowledge.

The activities in this chapter activate and stimulate the learners to think. Some of the activities are quite cognitively demanding. This helps students to consolidate their learning and use their imagination and reasoning skills.

5.1 True/False dictation

Aims	LANGUAGE	The alphabet (in Variation).
	OTHER	Critical listening; correcting sentences; translating.
Demo subject	BIOLOGY	
	TOPIC	The circulatory system
Alternative subjects	GEOGRAPHY	Landforms
	MATHEMATICS	Data handling
	BUSINESS STUDIES	People in business
	Any topic you want your students to be sure of	

Preparation

Write a set of true and false statements on a specific topic you want your students to revise.

Example

> **Biology   The circulatory system**
>
> 1 *The heart pumps blood through blood vessels (T)*
> 2 *The left side of the heart pumps the blood to the lungs (F)—right*
> 3 *When the blood contains lots of oxygen it turns bright red (T)*
> 4 *The left hand side of the heart is bigger than the right hand side (T)*
> 5 *There are 4 types of blood vessels (F) —3*
> 6 *Veins carry blood away from the heart (F) —to*

Procedure

1 Tell the students you are going to give them a dictation with a difference. You are going to dictate sentences to them in English to revise a particular topic. They have to decide if each sentence is true or false. If they think a sentence is true they have to translate it into the mother tongue and write it down. If they think it's false they rewrite the sentence in English so that it is true.

2 Tell the students you will read each sentence twice. The first time they just need to listen and decide if it is true or false.

3 Read out your sentences. For lower levels you could put some of the keywords on the board.

4 Check their sentences.

5 Ask the students to translate the true sentences they wrote in the mother tongue back into English. They should now have six true sentences written in their books on this particular topic.

Variation

If the sentences are true they write the sentence using just the first letter of each word.

Example   **Statement 1**

t h p b t b v

At the end of the activity they have to re-create the sentences using the letters as an *aide-mémoire*. They write the completed sentences in their notebooks. This is a nice way of getting students to re-write quite complicated sentences, and also of practising the sounds of the English alphabet.

Acknowledgements

This is adapted from an idea by Mario Rinvolucri.

5.2 Jumbled sentences

Aims   LANGUAGE   Word order; spelling.

         OTHER   Checking and matching descriptions to key words.

Demo subject   CHEMISTRY

         TOPIC   Chemical change

Alternative subjects   BUSINESS STUDIES   Production processes

         BIOLOGY   The composition, function and circulation of blood

         ICT   Graphics—creating images and image manipulation

Preparation

1 Choose a list of keywords.

2 Write one description for each key word and number it.

3 Write a jumbled version of each description.

Example   **Seven different types of chemical reaction**

Key words

Oxidation	Reduction	Decomposition
Exothermic	Endothermic	Neutralisation
Displacement.		

Descriptions

1 Oxygen usually combines with substances to make the oxide.
2 Oxygen is removed from a substance by another chemical.
3 Heat energy is used to break down a compound into simpler parts.
4 The reaction supplies the energy (as heat).
5 In these reactions energy has to be supplied from outside, usually as heat.
6 Acids react with bases, alkalis, reactive metals and carbonates.
7 A more reactive element displaces a less reactive element from its compound.

Examples of jumbled descriptions

Make sure you keep the capital letter to show where the sentence starts.

A energy reaction The supplies the (as heat).
B usually Oxygen oxide to with make substances combines the.

Procedure

1 Write the keywords all over the board. Give the students a few minutes to discuss them.

2 Dictate the correct descriptions in random order.

3 Ask the students to check their sentences with a partner and then match a keyword to each description. Check the matching is correct.

4 Read out the descriptions, one at a time, and ask volunteers to say the matching keywords.

5 Rub out the descriptions from the board. Ask the students to put their descriptions away.

6 Display one of the scrambled descriptions on the board, electronic whiteboard, or screen. Ask for a volunteer to come up and write the keyword on the board and then rewrite the matching sentence correctly. Explain that the capital letter starts the description. Continue in the same way until all the scrambled descriptions are rearranged. This is to anchor the description.

7 In pairs the students take each keyword and write brief examples, for example, *Endothermic Reaction—Photosynthesis—plants making their food.* The students read these examples out for you and the class to check.

5.3 Who or what am I?

Aims LANGUAGE Defining (see Appendix 2); comparing (see Appendix 2).

OTHER Recognizing and understanding key words; matching definitions with key words; listening; giving examples.

Materials Copies of word/definition sheets for the whole class.

Demo subject GEOGRAPHY

TOPIC Chemical weathering

Alternative subjects MATHEMATICS Shapes

LITERATURE Poets and their style of poetry

HISTORY Communication inventions

Preparation

1 Write a list of words you want your students to revise. Prepare two definitions for each word, one easy and one more detailed.

2 Write letters next to the easy definitions and numbers next to the more detailed definitions.

Example *hydrolysis A, 1   oxidation B, 2   hydration C, 3   solution D, 4   carbonation E, 5*

Hydrolysis

Definition A This process leads to the breakdown of felspars.

Definition 1 This is caused by a chemical reaction with the water which involves H and OH ions.

3 Write the words and definitions on a sheet and copy one for each student.

Procedure

1 Write on the board the words you want defined. Give the students time to write the words down and study them. Rub out the words from the board.

2   Tell the students that you are going to read out two definitions for each word. The first set of definitions you read will be detailed. You have given each definition in this set a different number.

3   Tell them that when you read these definitions they will not be in any particular order. When they hear the definition they guess which word it defines and write that number next to their chosen word.

4   Read out a definition and write its number on the board. Give the students time to think. Read the definition a second time and ask the students to write the number next to the word they think it defines. Read out a second definition and continue in the same way until all the words on your list have been covered.

5   Get students to check their answers with a partner.

6   Read the second list of definitions, the easier ones with the letters. The students listen and write the letter of the definition next to its word. Now they have a letter and a number next to each word.

7   Get students to check with their partners. Check the students have matched the correct definition numbers and letters with the right words.

8   Give out copies of the words and definitions.

Follow-up

The students work with a partner. They take it in turn to read out a word and its easy definition, then ask their partner, *Can you tell me something more about this, please?*

5.4   Guess my word

Aims   LANGUAGE   Describing (see Appendix 2).

OTHER   Guessing words.

Demo subject   SPORTS SCIENCE/PHYSICAL EDUCATION

TOPIC   Non-ball sports

Alternative subjects   CHEMISTRY   Physical changes

MUSIC   Names of baroque composers

GEOGRAPHY   Weather components

Key words for any subject

Procedure

1   Ask the students to think of a word on a particular topic. They mustn't say the word but must stand up when they have thought of it.

Example   **Non-ball sports**—*judo, swimming, running, high jump, aerobics, long jump, badminton, rowing*

2   Tell the class you are going to try to guess their word. If you say exactly their word they can sit down. The winner is the last person to be standing.

3 Have two columns on the board, one for the wrong guesses and another for the right ones. Make a guess and write the word in the appropriate column on the board.

4 As soon as you have made a right guess, the student(s) with that word sit down. It is now up to them to guess the words of the other students. Meanwhile you write all the guesses (right or wrong) on the board. Each time a student sits they join in with the rest of the class who are guessing.

5 If there are problems guessing the last few words, ask the students to tell you the first letter.

6 When all the words have been guessed ask the students to copy all the words from the board. i.e. the right and the wrong guesses.

7 Put the students into pairs. They take it in turns to describe one of the words so that their partner can guess which one it is. Give them some useful phrases such as *It's something that…, It's a kind of …, You use it for…-ing*. See Appendix 2.

Comments

Step 7 could be done in another lesson, or individually for homework.

Acknowledgements

This is adapted from an activity we learnt from Paul Davis.

5.5 A word beginning with …

Aims   LANGUAGE   Describing words (see Appendix 2); asking and answering questions; the letters of the alphabet.

         OTHER   Working in groups.

Materials   ONE SLIP OF PAPER PER STUDENT

Demo subject   Biology or Sports Science

         TOPIC   Bones, muscle types and structures

Alternative subjects   PHYSICS   The solar system

         HISTORY   Countries and leaders of the Soviet Union

         MUSIC   Different kinds of composition

         Any topic you want your students to revise

Procedure

1 Put the class into teams of not more than six. Write the names of the teams at the top of the board. Each team needs to appoint a questioner and an answerer.

2 Write on the board the topic you want to focus on.

Example   *Bones, muscle types and structures*

3 Ask the groups to write a list of as many words they can think of related to the topic. They can look in their books for help.

Example
skeletal muscle	hamstring	vertebra
cardiac muscle	tendons	femur
pectorals	deltoid	pelvis
abdominals	carpals	humerus
biceps	tarsals	ulna
quadriceps	scapula	

4 Check their lists.

5 Tell the class they are going quiz each other about their words. Put the following framework on the board and ask the class to give you some examples.

The name of a _____ *beginning with c.*

A _____ *beginning with p.*

A _____ *beginning with f.*

A _____ *which is a* _____ .

A word to do with _____ .

A word for a _____ *beginning with* _____ .

6 A questioner starts, using your framework. They can only use the words they have already written down. Explain that the other teams will have a short time to discuss the answer. When you give the signal, for example, clap, and **not** before, their answerers come to the board and write their answer under their team name.

7 Rub out any incorrect answers. Give a point for each correct answer.

8 Continue like this with a different team asking the question each time. A maximum of 12 words on the board will probably be enough.

9 Ask each team to write in their books a gapped description of each of the items they asked about.

Example *The* _____ *are muscles which move the arms and shoulders.*
(pectorals)

10 Rub out the words on the board. Now each team reads out their descriptions in random order. Give the groups time to agree on the missing word and then the answerers in each group write the word on the board. Give a point for each correct question, and each correct answer.

Variation

Step 9 could be a homework activity and step 10 could be done in another lesson.

5.6 Call our bluff

Aims   LANGUAGE Writing true/false statements.

          OTHER   Student–student dictation; working in groups; listening for specific information; remembering important facts; recording true information.

Materials Five slips of paper per group.

Demo subject FOOD TECHNOLOGY

              TOPIC Nutrition

Alternative subjects BIOLOGY Parts of a plant

              SPORTS SCIENCE Factors affecting performance

              HISTORY Different aspects of a historical period

              Any topic you want to revise

Preparation

Write a list of areas related to the topic you want your students to revise. Have one area per group.

Example **Nutrition**—*Areas: Carbohydrates, Proteins, Vitamins, Fats, Minerals*

Procedure

1 Put all the students into groups of about five. Give each group a different area of the topic to work on. Give each group a number or let them choose a name, and write these on the board.

2 Give out five slips of paper per group. Ask three people in each group to write the word 'true' on a slip of paper and the other two to write the word 'false'. They mix up their slips of paper and distribute them in their group.

3 The students with the 'true' slips each have to write a true sentence about the topic. The students with the 'false' slips each write a false sentence about the topic. They check their sentences with each other and then you.

4 The first group starts by reading out their sentences to the class. They read each one twice. The first time they read at normal speed, and the second time at dictation speed. The rest of the class listen the first time and individually decide if the statement is true or false. If they think it is true, they write it down with its number when they hear it the second time. They do **not** write the sentences they think are false.

5 The groups compare their sentences and agree on which ones they think are true. Each group in turn then tells the original group the numbers of the sentences they have agreed on. Write their numbers on the board under the name of the appropriate group. When all the groups have done this, the original group reads out their true sentences. Give each group one point for each true sentence they chose. All the class must make sure they have a written record of these true sentences, and have crossed out any false ones. In this way they will all have a copy of the correct information.

6 Repeat steps 4 and 5 till all the groups have read their sentences.

Variation

This could also be a teacher-generated activity if you read out sentences for students to identify and write down the true ones.

5.7 Add extra information

Aims LANGUAGE **Expressions of frequency.**

OTHER **Dictation practice; revision; retrieving and expanding information; working in groups.**

Materials **Overhead projector and screen, electronic whiteboard, or photocopied lists of frequency words.**

Demo subject BIOLOGY

TOPIC **Sexual reproduction in flowering plants**

Alternative subjects MATHEMATICS **Types of graphs**

GEOGRAPHY **Types of rivers**

BUSINESS STUDIES **External economic influences**

Preparation

1 Make a list of frequency words and copy it if necessary.

Example

> We can classify expressions of indefinite frequency on a scale from **always** to **never**, where always = 100% and never = 0%. These numbers are only a general indication, not exact values.
>
> 100% always
> 95% nearly always/almost always
> 90% usually/normally/generally
> 75% often/frequently
> 50% sometimes
> 40% occasionally
> 25% rarely/seldom
> 10% hardly ever
>   0% never

Photocopiable © Oxford University Press

2 Write a list of not more than five or six words related to the topic.

Example *inflorescence, calyx, corolla, androecium, gynaecium*

Procedure

1 Display the list of frequency words or write them on the board, and check that the students understand them in their mother tongue and English. Get the students to copy the list or give each student a photocopy of the frequency words.

2 Put the students into groups of fours. Each group chooses a secretary.

3 Explain that you will dictate a list of words related to the topic. The class will have time to discuss them before writing. Each group writes one sentence for each topic word using an expression of frequency to add useful information. Tell the students that only sentences which are appropriate and sensible will be accepted. Give examples on the board and highlight the frequency words.

Example *The calyx consists of sepals, which are **usually** green and small.*
*The gynaecium is **always** the female part of the flower.*

4 Dictate the list one word at a time. Set a time limit for discussion and writing. This depends on the level of the class.

5 Divide the board into columns, one for each topic word. Write one word at the top of each column and ask the groups to read out their sentences. Write these in the appropriate column. Get the class to discuss, agree or disagree with the sentences. At the end of the discussion get each student to write down the sentences they think are most useful.

5.8 Definition bingo

Aims LANGUAGE Understanding definitions (see Appendix 2).

OTHER Matching key words and definitions; listening; understanding and memorizing key words.

Materials Slips of paper or card; a bag or hat.

Demo subject CHEMISTRY

TOPIC Important substances and processes

Alternative subjects SPORTS SCIENCE Cardiovascular system

MATHEMATICS Different types of graphs

BUSINESS STUDIES Business ownership structures

Keywords for any topic you want to revise

Preparation

1 Prepare a list of nine key words you want your students to understand and remember.

2 Write a definition or description for each key word on a separate slip of paper or card. At lower levels write the descriptions in the mother tongue and in English.

Example

Keywords	Definitions
acid	A chemical compound which has a sour taste and will change litmus to red.
base	A chemical which can neutralize an acid.
synthesis	The joining together of elements to create compounds.
neutralize	Combine an acid with a base to produce salt and water.
evaporation	The process by which some parts of a liquid have enough energy to change into a gas at temperatures below the liquid's boiling point.
compound	Material made from atoms of different elements.
molecule	The combination of two or more atoms chemically joined together to form a compound.
experiment	A planned test which gives evidence for or against a scientific idea.
alkali	A chemical compound which contains hydroxide ions and can be dissolved in water. It will turn litmus blue.
electrolysis	The separation of elements in a chemical compound by electricity.
catalyst	A substance which speeds up a chemical reaction but which itself remains unchanged and can be used again.
element	A substance containing one atom which cannot be broken down into other substances by chemical reactions.

Procedure

1 Write the key words all over the board.

2 Ask the students to draw a nine-square grid. Tell them to choose nine of the keywords and to write each one in a square, in any order.

3 Put your definitions into a bag or a hat. Pull out one at a time and read it out. At lower levels read the mother tongue and the English description. If the students have the matching word on their grids, they cross it out. When a student has crossed out a whole line of words, he or she calls out *Line!* The line could be vertical, horizontal or diagonal. Get them to read out their words and to give the meanings.

4 Continue reading the definitions until one student has crossed out all their squares. This student calls out *Full House!*, then reads out one of their words, asking someone else in the class to give its meaning. Continue like this until all that student's words have been read out.

5 Read out any definitions still remaining in your bag and ask students to give you the matching word.

6 Ask the class to write the key words and definitions in their books. They could also add the mother tongue equivalents.

5.9 On target

Aims LANGUAGE Spelling practice.

OTHER Expanding and consolidating topic vocabulary; remembering and revising information.

Materials A stopwatch or egg-timer; sheets of paper.

Demo subject MUSIC

TOPIC Musical instruments

Alternative subjects BIOLOGY Names of bones, muscles, enzymes in digestive juices, names of human arterial system, parts of the heart etc.

GEOGRAPHY Rivers, capital cities, mountain ranges, islands

ICT Input devices

Vocabulary for any subject

Preparation

1 Find or write lists of six words related to each topic.

Musical instruments

List A Brass instruments: bugle, cornet, euphonium, trumpet, tuba, flugelhorn.

List B Wind instruments: flute, clarinet, piccolo, saxophone, oboe, bagpipes.

List C Percussion instruments: bongo, castanets, glockenspiel, triangle, xylophone, marimba

List D Stringed instruments: cello, guitar, harp, balalaika, zither, violin.

Procedure

1   Put the students into team groups. Each team has one sheet of writing paper and chooses a writer. Change the team writer after each round.

2   Explain the rules of the game. Write a topic on the board. Tell the class you have a list of six words about that topic. Each team must write down six words they think could be on your list. Set an appropriate time limit for each round. When the time limit is up, the students hold up their paper. No more writing is allowed.

3   Ask a group to read out one of their words. Start each round with a different group. If a team calls out a word which is on your list, write that word on one side of the board in one colour, for example, red. The team scores a point. If the word is not on your list write it on the other side of the board in a different colour, blue. Continue round the teams until all your words have been called out. If at the end there are words left on your list, which have not been called out, then write these up on the board in red.

4   All the teams score a point for each word they match with your list, but **only** for the words on your list. The teams keep their scores. With the students, check the blue word list and reject any you and they feel do not fit in with the topic list. The students copy down the appropriate words from the lists.

5   Begin again with a new topic and a new list.

Acknowledgements

This idea is an adaptation of a family party game.

5.10 Questions to answers

Aims   LANGUAGE Writing *what is/what are* questions; writing definitions (see Appendix 2).

OTHER   Listening; understanding definitions.

Demo Subject MATHEMATICS

Alternative MUSIC The different notes
subjects
CHEMISTRY Chemical reactions

LITERATURE Different kinds of poetry

Any definitions you want your students to focus on.

Preparation

Write a set of short definitions related to previous work.

Procedure

1   Tell the class you are going to read out some answers to questions. Their task is to write a *What is/What are* question which would elicit this answer. They must **not** write down the answer.

2 Read out the first definition, and write the first two words on the board. Give students time to write the question individually. Then check the questions to make sure they understand what to do.

3 Continue in the same way with the remaining answers, but do not check them yet. Ask students to leave a line after each of their questions.

4 In pairs they compare their questions. Then you check their questions.

5 Ask the students to reconstruct each of your answers and write it after its question.

6 Using the information in the questions and answers, the students write a definition for each keyword.

Example You read the definitions and your students have to write the questions.

---

1 A number that can't be divided by anything, except itself.
Q What is a prime number?
2 A number that doesn't divide by 2.
Q What is an odd number?
3 A shape with four equal sides.
Q What is a square?
4 Triangles which have two equal sides and two equal angles.
Q What are isosceles triangles?
5 A part of ten written by putting a point or comma before the number.
Q What is a decimal?
6 Fractions that are equal in value even though they look different.
Q What are equivalent fractions?

Photocopiable © Oxford University Press

5.11 Mastermind

Aims   LANGUAGE Giving short answers; writing questions
(see Appendix 2).

OTHER   Critical listening; checking understanding.

Demo subject   ART

TOPIC The Renaissance Painters

Alternative   PHYSICS Electric current in circuits
subjects
MATHEMATICS Calculations

HISTORY A historical character

Any topic you want to revise

Preparation

Write a list of about eight questions on a previously taught topic.
They should be questions which elicit fairly short answers.

Example

The Renaissance painters

1 Name an Italian painter from this period.
2 Name an English painter from this period.
3 Name a German painter from this period.
4 Name an important picture from this period.
5 What period followed this period?
6 What were their favourite materials?
7 What kind of pictures did they paint?
8 What are the dates of this period?

Photocopiable © Oxford University Press

Procedure

1 Ask two students to come to the front of the class. These could be
volunteers, or you may want to choose them. Explain that they are
going to be the 'experts'. They will have to work together to tell the
class the answers to your questions.

2 Get the rest of the class to write the numbers 1–8 down the side
of a page.

3 Tell the class you are going to ask the 'experts' eight questions. The
class have to listen to their answers and decide if they are right or
wrong. They put a tick or a cross next to the matching question
number in their books. You need to do the same.

4 Ask the experts the questions, and check that the class are marking
the experts' answers right or wrong. Then let the experts sit down
and relax!

5 Write the numbers 1–8 on the board. Go through the questions and count the number of ticks and crosses from the class for each one. In this way you will get feedback about how much understanding or misunderstanding there is! It also gives feedback to the students as to the areas they need to revise.

6 Repeat the questions which the 'experts' answered correctly and get different students to write on the board the correct answers that they heard from the 'experts'.

7 Now repeat the questions which were answered incorrectly and invite students to tell you the right answer. They write these on the board.

8 Ask the class to copy all the answers into their books, leaving a line after each one.

9 Ask the students to re-write in their books the questions to the answers. This could be done for homework.

5.12 Ask me again

Aims   LANGUAGE   Consolidating question forms; answering questions; translating.

OTHER   Memorizing important concepts.

Demo subject   GEOGRAPHY

TOPIC   Natural features

Alternative subjects   BUSINESS STUDIES   A Human Resources Manager, a CEO, a profit and loss account

MUSIC   A violin, a clarinet, a harpsichord

CHEMISTRY   A compound, an element, a gas

Any topic you want your students to revise

Preparation

1 Make a list of three questions for key concepts you want your students to be able to describe.

Example   *What is an estuary?*
What is a glacier?
What is a desert?

2 Think of a number of possible answers in the mother tongue for one of these questions. It's a good idea to choose the most difficult one.

Procedure

1 Give your students your question and ask them to repeat it after you so that you can check their pronunciation.

2 Tell them they are going to ask you this question again and again. They will ask the question in English and you will answer in the mother tongue. The idea of this repetition is for them to consolidate the question forms.

Example   SS *What is an estuary?*
T   (in mother tongue) a piece of water

SS *What is an estuary?*
T   (in mother tongue) the wide part of a river

SS *What is an estuary?*
T   (in mother tongue) a place where fresh water meets salt water

SS *What is an estuary?*
T   (in mother tongue) a bay or inlet often at the mouth of river

SS *What is an estuary?*
T   (in mother tongue) a place where a river meets the sea

SS *What is an estuary?*
T   (in mother tongue) a tidal area

3   Ask the class to write in English all the answers they can remember. They can do this alone, in pairs or in a group. Then go through their information.

4   Put the students into pairs, student A and B. If you have multiple mother tongues in your class, put students sharing the same mother tongue together. Give student A one of your chosen questions and B the other. Tell them to prepare individually at least four answers to their question. They do this in the mother tongue. Give them a time limit.

5   When they have written their answers they give their question to their partner. Student A starts by asking student B's question, and student B answers in the mother tongue. student A repeats the question at least four times.

6   Together they reconstruct student B's answers into English. Invite one pair to write their information on the board, and then other pairs to add to it.

7   Repeat the activity with student B asking student A's question.

Comments

Students often have problems formulating questions. This is an effective way of helping them to memorize a question as a chunk of language.

Acknowledgements

This is an adaptation of 'One question—many answers', from *Grammar in Action Again,* Frank and Rinvolucri, Prentice Hall International, 1991.

5.13 Three things I know about …

Aims   LANGUAGE   Defining (see Appendix 2); asking for and giving information

OTHER   Revising and expanding information on a subject; working in a group; note-taking.

Materials   Large sheets of paper—one for each topic; sheets of paper—one for every student; a stick-on label for every student.

Demo subject   BIOLOGY

TOPIC   The human body: the skeleton, muscles, air supply, circulatory system, cells, digestive system, reproductive system

Alternative subjects   SPORT   Equipment and rules required for any sport

HISTORY   The Renaissance period—writers, thinkers and artists

DESIGN AND TECHNOLOGY   Metals—joining metals, reforming metal, heat treatment, best use of standard components for metal

Preparation

Write a list of topics you want the students to revise.

Procedure

1 Divide the class into groups of three or four. Give each group a topic they have studied recently. Give each student a label. All students write their topic title on a label and stick it on themselves.

2 Ask each group to discuss three things they know about the subject. Give each student a sheet of paper and ask each to write down the three things the group has discussed.

3 Tell the students to find a partner from another group. The pairs take turns to read out their lists and ask their partner for one more piece of information about the topic. They write the extra piece of information about their topic on their own sheet of paper. Then they move on to new partners until they have collected four or five more pieces of information.

4 The students go back to their original group to read and assess all the information they have collected, i.e. they pool it. You check the information.

5 Ask each group to write three or four sentences about their topic.

6 Each group reads their sentences to the rest of the class. The other students make notes.

7 Write one topic title at the top of each large sheet of paper, for example, 'Circulatory system'. Pin up the sheets. The groups go round these topic sheets and write on them any information they can remember. They can use their notes.

8 Take the large sheets and pin them on the board. Read out the information. The students write notes in their exercise books for future reference. This final check helps to fix and anchor the information in their minds.

5.14 Give me four

Aims   LANGUAGE   Discussion and agreement; facts and figures.

OTHER   Note-taking; thinking and writing at speed; working in a group; revising key points.

Materials   A sheet of paper for each group; a set of question sheets.

Demo subject   GEOGRAPHY

TOPIC   Use and abuse of the environment

Alternative subjects   HISTORY   Conflicts and treaties

BUSINESS STUDIES   Quality and control procedures

FOOD TECHNOLOGY   Properties of ingredients

Preparation

1 Write a selection of typical questions on the topic. Duplicate the question sheet, one for each student.

2 Summarize the questions and write a short list of four key points you would expect the students to include when answering each of the questions. Turn your key points into questions, see the examples below:

Examples

> 1 Give me four key points, including facts and figures, that you would include in an answer about acid rain.
>
> 2 Give me four key points, including facts and figures, that you would include in an answer about ecosystems.
>
> 3 Give me four key points you would include in an answer about the use and abuse of water.
>
> 4 Give me four key points for the use and abuse of land.
>
> 5 Give me four reasons why deserts are expanding.
>
> 6 Give me four reasons for global warming.

Procedure

1 Put the students into groups and give out one sheet of paper per group. Number or name the groups and write these numbers or names on the board. The group members take it in turns to be the writer for each round of the activity.

2 Tell the students that this is a race. Each group must give their writer a list of four answers for each question. Remind them to whisper their answers to the writer.

3 Tell them that the first group to finish their list should all stand up at the same time. Explain that as soon as a group stands up, the activity stops, no more writing.

4 The fastest group reads out their list. Other students can question and challenge the answers. If the list is acceptable the group gets 4 marks. You are the final judge. Write the score on the board under the group number or name. If the list has been challenged successfully and only three examples remain correct, for example, then the group only gets the score for the accepted number.

5 The other groups then give extra examples. If these are correct they get a mark for each one. Write the scores for the other groups on the board. If different groups have the same extra examples they all get a mark.

6 Continue the activity. The group with the most marks at the end wins.

7 Give out the question sheets and discuss them. They can be used for homework.

6

Using supplementary resources

The more we encourage our students to research their information and share it with each other, the more independent they will become. Using visuals and technical equipment adds another dimension to our teaching and appeals to different learning styles. We need to encourage our students to go to more than one source of information. As much of the Internet is in English this is a useful tool for CLIL. What is more, researching information from the Internet may be an important skill for their future working life. A useful reference book for using the Internet is *The Internet*, OUP (see Appendix 3).

In this chapter there is a mix of activities using the Internet, film, or pictures. When using the Internet, we have sometimes suggested doing the research at school but it could always be done at home if that is possible for your students. If they do not have access to the Internet at school you could print off some relevant material for them and let them do their research with hard copy.

One valuable outcome of getting students to do their own research is the follow-up, where they share what they have discovered and teach each other. Activities such as 6.6, 'Go and find out', and 6.7, Concentric circles', are examples of this. In 6.10, 'Vote for ours!', students have to prepare a presentation. 6.4, 'Answer my picture questions', and 6.5, 'It's my life', require them to ask and answer questions.

Using visuals is another way of giving input. 6.1, 'Reading the picture', encourages students to use their imagination. In 6.2, 'Visual dictation', students have to draw their own picture and 6.3, 'Group visuals and gap-fills', makes use of a chart.

All these activities lead into students talking to each other, teaching each other, and sharing their information. This is a natural way to encourage our students to speak about their subject.

6.1 Reading the picture

Aims LANGUAGE Defining (see Appendix 2); cause and result
(see Appendix 2); conditionals; modals; questions
(see Appendix 2).

OTHER Interpreting visuals, charts and diagrams; writing
comments and questions.

Materials Atlases or maps and paper.

Demo subject GEOGRAPHY

TOPIC Map reading

Alternative subjects Any which use diagrams and visuals

Preparation

1 Choose two countries or regions you want your students to study.
Find one map for each country or region and note the page
references in their atlases.

2 Make your own list of the key information you want the students to
extract from each map.

3 Write some example questions to put on the board.

Procedure

1 Put the students into groups of four. Give two of the students the
letter A and the other two the letter B.

2 Give each pair a sheet of paper and ask them to write their names at
the top. Give each pair the page reference of the map you want them
to look at first: all As have one page, all Bs the other one.

3 Tell the pairs that you want them to look at the map and to write a
question about it that they would like the other pair to answer. The
questions can be assumptions rather than factual information found
on the map. Write examples of questions on the board to help the
students get started.

Examples A *What colour is used to show the peaks of very high mountains?*
B *Do you think this area has a high or low population?*
C *What do you see at grid reference…?*
D *What kind of work do you think most of the people do in this area?*

The pairs look at the map and together make up a question which
they write on their sheet of paper. Then the pairs exchange their
maps and question sheets.

4 Now the pairs discuss and write down an answer to the question.
They study the new map and together make up another question
which they write down under their answer. The pairs pass the maps
and question sheets back. By exchanging the sheets continuously
they build up questions and answers about both maps.

5   Set a time limit depending on the ability of the class and the amount of information you think the students will be able to extract. At the end of the set time the four students in each group check the two maps together and discuss their questions and answers. As a group they add any further information and challenge any of the answers.

6   Divide the board into two sections, one for each map. Write the titles or references at the top of the two board sections. Ask the students to read out a question for the rest of the class to discuss and check. The students make notes.

7   Write any unanswered or problem questions on the board and discuss them. Add any key information from your list which you feel should be included. The students make a copy of the notes on the board.

Comments

For useful websites for different subjects see Appendix 4.

6.2 Visual dictation

Aims LANGUAGE Defining key words (see Appendix 2); spatial language. (see Appendix 2); asking and answering questions (see Appendix 2); the letters of the alphabet.

OTHER Revising words; using charts and diagrams; using the visual intelligence.

Demo subject BUSINESS STUDIES

TOPIC Maslow's Hierarchy of Needs

Alternative subjects FOOD TECHNOLOGY Mind map of different food groups according to their nutrition

RELIGIOUS STUDIES Histogram of number of people of different religions in a particular continent

BIOLOGY Classification of plants and animals, picture of the heart

Any topic which is demonstrated with a visual

Preparation

1   Prepare a dictation of the chart you want your students to understand and remember.

2   Write a list of the language they will need to understand.

Procedure

1   Tell the students the topic and ask them to tell you what they know about it.

2   Go through the language you will be using in the dictation, for example spatial language (see Appendix 2).

3   Dictate the diagram, spelling out any words they need to write.

4   Let the students compare notes with the people near them and ask you if they have any differences.

Maslow's Hierarchy of Needs

Draw a large equilateral triangle. Using a ruler, divide it into five equal horizontal sections. Write in each section as follows: in the bottom section write 'Physical Survival', in the next section 'Safety', in the middle one 'Love and belonging', in the next 'Self-esteem', and in the top one 'Self-actualization'.

Write the following under your triangle:

Maslow believed that we are all motivated by the same things. These needs are in order of priority and the lower level ones at the bottom of the triangle must be achieved before the higher needs can be met.

5 As a whole class the students now take it in turns to dictate the diagram back to you. They need to include the words inside the triangle and the text underneath. You draw and write on the board exactly what they say.

6 Put the students into five groups, allocate one of the hierarchies to each group and ask them to translate the heading into their language. They then discuss what they think it means.

7 Each group tells the class their translation and interpretation. You add anything they have left out. Everyone takes notes.

6.3 Group visuals and gap-fills

Aims　LANGUAGE　Defining and describing (see Appendix 2).

　　　　　OTHER　　Gap-filling; using graphs, charts and diagrams; using other sources for research; revision; working on subject-related charts, graphs, diagrams.

Demo subject　MATHEMATICS

　　　　　TOPIC　Shapes

Alternative subjects　BIOLOGY　The skeleton, a diagram of the skull of a dog with arrows pointing to the parts to be labelled

　　　　　GEOGRAPHY　Map reading signs, symbols and definitions

　　　　　ART　Schools of painting, artist's name or picture, name or visual of example paintings

Preparation

1　Make a list of shapes you want the students to revise and research.

2　Make two worksheets as in the examples in Worksheets 6.3a and 6.3b.

3　Make a large copy of each worksheet so that you can display them to the whole class. Either make copies for the whole class or ask the students to draw the grid at steps 1 and 4.

Worksheet 6.3a		
Number of sides	Name of polygon	Draw the shape
	Triangle	
4	Quadrilateral	
5		

Photocopiable © Oxford University Press

Worksheet 6.3b

Number of sides	Name of polygon	Draw the shape
	Hexagon	
	Octagon	
10	Decagon	

Procedure

Lesson 1

1 Display the first worksheet and ask the students to copy it.
2 Ask them to work in pairs to fill in the missing information.
3 Ask for volunteers to give the answers.
4 Show the students the second worksheet and repeat the activity.
5 Allocate one shape to each pair, and ask them to find out as much extra information about their shape as they can for homework using different research sources, for example: formulae, symmetry, where the shape can be found in the natural world or in architecture. Encourage students to find visuals.

Lesson 2

Each pair writes a report about their findings and gives a short presentation.

Variation

The pairs design and prepare a poster about their shape, including pictures/photographs/drawings plus written information. These are displayed.

6.4 Answer my picture questions

Aims   LANGUAGE   Practising question forms (see Appendix 2).

OTHER   Using different resources; student–student input; getting new information.

Materials   Copies of the chosen visuals—one per group; and texts—one per student; different coloured board pens.

Demo subject   HISTORY

TOPIC   Hannibal crossing the Alps in 281BC

Alternative Subjects   PHYSICS   Using waves—diagrams and graphs

ITC   Data storage—diagrams

GEOGRAPHY   Climate—graphs and weather charts

Preparation

1   Find a short text from the Internet, a textbook, or an encyclopaedia, and a visual you could use to go with the text. In this example you could use the Internet for the text and any picture of the journey, even a famous painting, for example, Joseph Turner—*Snow Storm: Hannibal Crossing the Alps*.

2   Make a copy of the text and another of the picture. Remove any labels from the picture. If there is any writing or information such as titles outside the frame, cut it off. Leave just the picture.

3   You will be dividing the class into A and B groups. The A groups will need a visual per group. The B groups will need copies of the text. Make enough copies of the text for each student in the class.

4   You may need to simplify the language of the text depending on the level of the class. Write line reference numbers on the text before you photocopy it.

Hannibal crosses the Alps (218 BC)

Some details of Hannibal's crossing still exist. The first danger came from the Allobroges, who attacked the rear of Hannibal's column of soldiers and animals. Then Hannibal was attacked again by other Celtic groups. These attackers rolled heavy stones down the mountainsides onto the soldiers and animals below. This made the animals and soldiers panic and many of them fell from the narrow, dangerous paths to their deaths. Others were crushed and horribly injured. Hannibal lost many men and animals. There were constant attacks throughout the journey.

Hannibal could not trust his Gallic guides and this made it even more difficult. Hannibal bivouacked on large bare rocks to cover the passage by night of his horses and pack animals in the gorges below. Snow was falling, it was very, very cold, and the soldiers and animals were wet, hungry and frightened. Very often landslides blocked the narrow tracks and a lot of time was lost just trying to clear the paths.

Finally on the 15th day, after a journey of five months from Cartagena, with 20,000 foot soldiers, 6,000 cavalry and only a few of the original 38 elephants, Hannibal arrived in Italy.

Photocopiable © Oxford University Press

Procedure

1 Divide the class into equal-sized A and B groups.

2 Explain the difference between open and closed questions and ask the students to use both kinds of questions:

An open question is general and can have a variety of answers. Open questions about the picture can include not only what people see in the picture but also what they imagine, feel about or associate with the picture—thinking outside the frame. A closed question can be a '*yes/no*' question and usually has only one answer.

Example An open question: *What things would make the journey across the Alps so difficult?*
A closed question: *What were the dates of the Second Punic War?*

3 Give the A groups the visuals and the B groups the texts. Tell the B groups to read the text for general understanding, i.e. to get the gist. They do not have to understand all the words.

4 Tell the A groups to study the visuals and write a list of questions they would like answered when looking at the visual. Ask them to use both open and closed questions. Set the same time limit for the reading and question writing.

5 Ask the A groups to pair up with a B group and show and ask them their questions. The B groups scan the text and discuss possible answers for the open questions. The A groups make notes.

6   Display copies of the visual round the room. Let the text group (B) students walk round and look at them. Give them a few minutes to do this before they go back to their groups.

7   As a whole class and taking it in turns, the A groups ask their questions aloud and the B groups respond with answers. Write down a selection of the questions on the board for the students to copy.

8   Give out the rest of the text copies so that each student has a copy. Individually the students scan the text and underline any words or expressions they find difficult. Check and explain.

9   The students copy the questions from the board. As homework they write answers for as many of the questions as they can.

Comments

For useful websites see Appendix 4.

6.5 It's my life

Aims LANGUAGE Asking and answering questions (see Appendix 2); present perfect.

OTHER Researching using a variety of resources; cooperative learning; note-taking.

Materials Large sheets of card—one for each group.

Demo subject MUSIC

TOPIC 20th Century composers

Alternative subjects HISTORY 20th Century world leaders

SCIENCE Famous scientists and their discoveries

BUSINESS STUDIES Biographies of famous entrepreneurs

Preparation

Write a list of eight 20th century composers you want researched.

Procedure

Lesson 1

1   Write the names of the composers on the board. Put the students into eight groups and allocate the name of a composer to each group.

2   Explain to the students that they have a few days to find information about the composer. They can surf the Internet, check textbooks, journals and so on either at home or at school.

3   Tell the groups that they have to prepare a visual aid on a large piece of card with key biographical points, pictures and references. Each group also has to prepare a short gap-fill activity, with an answer sheet, about their composer. Check the gap-fills before the next lesson. Duplicate the gap-fill activities but not the answer sheets. For each student you will need one copy showing all the gap-fills. If possible the students download examples of the music to play to the class later.

Lesson 2

1 Give the groups time to prepare their visual aids and a short presentation about their composer. Explain that you want them to give the presentation in the first person, that is, as if they were the composer. Set a time limit for the presentations, for example two or three minutes each, depending on the ability of the students.

2 Say, *Let me introduce you to X,* and choose one of the composers from your list. The group representing that composer go to the front of the class and give their presentation. The other students ask questions and make notes. If the group have downloaded music give them extra time at the end of their presentation to play it.

3 Each group gives their presentation in the same way.

4 Display the group visual aids around the room. Students circulate and read what the other groups have written. They note websites and other reference points.

5 Give out copies of the gap-fill activities. The students fill these in for homework.

Lesson 3

1 Each group pins the answer sheet to their gap-fill activity next to their visual aid.

2 The students walk round and check their answers. In a small classroom this might have to be done group by group, or with just a couple at a time.

6.6 Go and find out

Aims	LANGUAGE Asking and answering questions (see Appendix 2).
Materials	Access to Internet; slips of paper—one per pair or student.
Other	Researching new information; note-taking; using the Internet.
Demo subject	FOOD TECHNOLOGY
	TOPIC Food processing
Alternative subjects	LITERATURE The Enlightenment period
	MATHEMATICS Trigonometry
	ICT Creating websites

Preparation

1 Choose a topic and find some relevant websites.

2 Write notes on the important points you want to be covered.

Procedure

1 Write on the board the topic you want your students to work on.

2 Give each student (or pair of students) a slip of blank paper. Ask them, alone or in pairs, to write a *wh-* question related to the topic. It must not be a *yes/no* question. You may need to remind them of the *wh-* question forms they will need.

Examples   *What is the definition of food processing?*
How is food processed?
How long does it take to process food?
Name three different ways of processing food
Name two ways preserving food.
Why do we process food?

3 They exchange questions with another student or pair.

4 Write some useful websites on the board (see Appendix 4). Tell them they need to go to the Internet and find the answer to the question they have been given.

5 Students get together with the students who gave them their question. They tell each other their answers, and take notes on the answers they hear.

6 Students read out the questions they wrote and the answers they have been given. The rest of the class take notes.

7 Let the class add any further information on the topic. Fill in any important gaps.

Comments

This could be done over two lessons with the Internet research taking place for homework.

6.7 Concentric circles

Aims   LANGUAGE Asking and answering questions (see Appendix 2).

OTHER   Note-taking; using a variety of resources to collect and revise information; finding, filtering, downloading, sorting and storing information.

Materials   Slips of paper—one per student; sheets of paper.

Demo subject   RELIGIOUS STUDIES

TOPIC World religions

Alternative subjects   GEOGRAPHY Any country; its industry, exports, cities, physical features

CHEMISTRY Simple chemical reactions and experiments

PHYSICS Sounds and how they are measured

Preparation

1 Write a list of eight world religions.

2 Prepare slips of paper with the name of a different world religion written on each one. Prepare one slip of paper for each student. Repeat the religions according to the size of the class. Do not include the statistics.

Example *In order of size: Christianity 2.1 billion, Islam 1.3 billion, Hinduism 900 million, Buddhism 376 million, Sikhism 23 million, Judaism 14 million, Shinto 4 million, Scientology 500 thousand.*

Procedure

Lesson 1

1 Give each student a religion slip. Ask the students to get together with others who have the same religion slip.

2 Tell the groups that they have to find out as much as they can about that religion. This could be done at school or at home. Set a time limit for the research, which should include useful reference sources and websites. The group information should be checked by you before the following lesson.

Lesson 2

1 In their groups each student has a few minutes to write brief notes and reference sources at the top of a sheet of paper which they can take with them to use during the activity. These notes should only be a few sentences long. Explain that students will use the rest of the sheet to write down the information they get from others.

2 Give each religion a letter. Get the students to write down their religion letter at the top of their paper.

Example

A Christianity	D Buddhism	G Shinto
B Islam	E Sikhism	H Scientology
C Hinduism	F Judaism	

Put the students into concentric circles, inner and outer, facing a partner. Each inner circle is made up of an A, B, C, and D student. The outer circle is made up of an E, F, G, and H student.

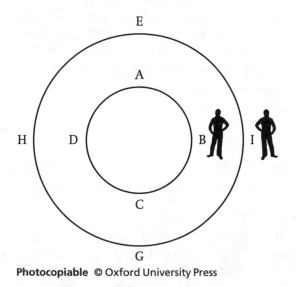

3 The students have a few minutes to tell their partners all they can about their researched religion. The partners make notes and ask questions. If the students cannot answer a question they write it down.

4 Stop the activity and tell students A, B, C and D to stay where they are. Students E, F, G and H move one place to their left. Repeat the activity.

5 Repeat the activity twice more, but ask the students to try to give the information without using their notes. Continue until they are all facing their original partners.

6 All the students return to their original research groups. Write any unanswered questions on the board. These can be checked for homework and answered in a following lesson.

7 The students discuss and construct mind maps to show the information they received about the other religions. Each student makes a copy to keep as reference.

Example   Hinduism

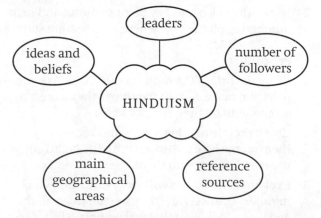

Photocopiable © Oxford University Press

8 Using the mind maps the students write a brief summary about each religion and a graph showing their comparative sizes.

9 Pin up a sheet entitled 'Useful references' and ask the students to write on it the resources they found in Lesson 1. This could be photocopied later for reference.

10 The students choose three religious leaders and note the reference points. As homework they check out the resource references and websites.

Follow-up

Groups of students give mini presentations about a particular religious leader.

Comments

For useful websites see Appendix 4.

6.8 What we hear and what we see

Aims LANGUAGE Listening for keywords and topic related expressions.

OTHER Cooperative learning; working in pairs; using video as input; predicting.

Materials Recorded films or video clips; sheets of paper.

Demo subject GEOGRAPHY

TOPIC The Oceans

Alternative subjects Any subject, using film or video which accompanies or complements a study course.

Preparation

1 View the video clip before using it in class and make notes on the subject matter and any key vocabulary. The video should not be more than ten minutes long.

2 Divide the video into key point sections, and make a note of the numbering on the tape where each section starts and finishes.

Procedure

1 Write the title of the topic on the board. Ask your students to work in pairs and make a list of the things they expect to see on the video and any vocabulary they expect to hear.

2 Check their lists of key words and vocabulary and write some of them on the board. Also write on the board any words you need to pre-teach and explain them.

3 Explain that the class will see a video clip which will last about ten minutes. The first time they see the video all they have to do is watch and listen. Tell them that you will play the video again but in short sections. These instructions could be given in the mother tongue.

4 Play the complete video. Try not to comment on the video as the idea is for the students to rely on each other rather than on you.

5 Get the students to write the word 'See' at the top of one page, and 'Hear' at the top of another. Divide the students into two groups—A and B. Tell all the A students to focus on things they see in the video and the B students to focus on everything they hear. When you pause the video they should make notes. They do not have to write in full sentences.

6 Play the video again, this time in sections, pausing to let the students write their words and brief notes.

7 Put students into groups of As and groups of Bs. The groups discuss, exchange information, and note key words and expressions. Each student makes their own notes.

8 Put the students into pairs, one A with one B. They compare and discuss their notes, with the A ('See') students building up a 'Hear' section of notes, and vice versa.

9 Ask the pairs to read out what they saw and what they heard. Write these on the board. If any key points, words or expressions have not been covered write them on the board and explain them. The students add these to their notes.

10 For homework the students find a written reference source for the topic and write a short paragraph about it, including any interesting extra information.

Follow-up

When the paragraphs have been checked they are copied and displayed. Write any particularly good reference sources on the board for the students to copy.

6.9 Give me my name and draw me

Aims LANGUAGE Describing and defining (see Appendix 2); comparing and contrasting (see Appendix 2); stating purposes and uses; *wh*-questions; order of adjectives; prepositions.

OTHER Sharing information; recognizing important items, signs and symbols; drawing conclusions (see Appendix 2); learning and revising vocabulary.

Materials A collection of visuals of apparatus or the real objects; sheets of paper; copies of diagrams for each student.

Demo subject SCIENCE

TOPIC Laboratory equipment

Alternative subjects GEOGRAPHY Map reading signs, symbols and grid references

BUSINESS STUDIES Commercial and Industrial signs, symbols and processes

FOOD TECHNOLOGY Processing and cooking food—charts showing treatment, reason, symbols and examples

Preparation

1 Collect visuals of apparatus and/or real objects.

2 Find or draw two diagrams of different experiments. The diagrams should show the title of the experiment and the procedure. These diagrams should be short and simple.

3 Write a list of the apparatus.

Example beaker, Bunsen burner, boss, clamp and stand, conical flask, evaporating basin, filter funnel, gauze, measuring cylinder, spatula, test tube, thermometer, triangle, tripod, litmus paper, bell jar, Petri dish, scales

4 Label the diagrams A and B. Copy the diagrams, making an A and a B for each student.

Procedure

Lesson 1

1 Write the title 'Laboratory equipment' on the board. Ask the students to work in pairs and write down, in English or in their mother tongue, as many examples as they can. Ask the students to read out their examples. Write them on the board. Translate where necessary. Add any missing pieces of equipment from your list.

2 Write the preferred order of adjectives on the board. Describe one piece of equipment to the class, using several adjectives in the preferred order.

Example **Order of adjectives**

Size Shape Colour Origin Material Use Noun

Ask the students to work individually and, using the order of adjectives to help them, to write a short description of another item without giving its name. Explain that they do not have to use all the adjective types.

3 Ask for volunteers to read out their descriptions while the others guess what it is. Show the visual of the described item. Write the description on the board under the order of adjectives, for example

Example

Size	Shape	Colour	Origin	Material	Use	Noun
A small	*cylindrical*	*transparent*	*—*	*glass*	*testing*	*?*

4 The students copy the examples. Clear the board of visuals and descriptions.

5 In pairs, and using their notes, the students take it in turn to describe pieces of apparatus for their partners to guess.

Lesson 2

1 Give out the copies of the experiments. Student As get diagram A and student Bs get diagram B. Tell the students not to show their partner the diagram. Give them time to look at the diagram and read the experiment.

2 Student A names the pieces of apparatus, and the Bs draw the items in their exercise books or on a separate sheet of paper. Then the As dictate the title and procedure of the experiment which the Bs write down.

3 Repeat the activity for the A students to do the drawing and writing.

4 The students compare their drawings and notes. Give out the extra copies so that all the students have copies of both experiments for reference.

6.10 Vote for ours!

Aims	LANGUAGE	Superlatives—the most… (see Appendix 2).
	OTHER	Listening; note-taking; giving a presentation; researching new information.
Materials		Access to Internet and reference books (in English or the mother tongue).
Demo subject	CHEMISTRY	
	TOPIC	The most important elements
Alternative subjects	FOOD TECHNOLOGY	The most important food properties
	LITERATURE	The most influential writers
	GEOGRAPHY	The most important rivers
		Any topic you want your students to research

Preparation

Make a list of the elements you want your students to research—one per group.

Procedure

1   Put the students into groups. You will need one group per element. Write the names of the elements on the board. Give the groups time to tell each other what they know about these elements.

2   Allocate one element per group, or let them choose one. Tell the class they are going to have a competition to see which is the most important element. Their task is to research all the information they can about their element. They can use the Internet and books. Give them some useful websites (see Appendix 4).

3   Put the following language on the board:

Vote for ours because…
You can't live without our element because…
This element is the King of Elements.
No other element is as important as…
This element is the most…

4   Tell the groups they are going to present the information to the other groups in a way which will convince them that their element is the most important. They can use some of the language on the board in their presentation. At the end of each presentation the groups give it a mark out of ten. The group with the most marks wins.

5   In their groups they make notes of everything they can remember about the other elements.

6.11 Visual dictation

Aims   LANGUAGE   Defining and describing (see Appendix 2); stating purposes and uses.

         OTHER   Scanning a text; reading and listening; recognizing important signs and symbols; interpreting diagrams, charts, graphs; learning and revising vocabulary.

Materials   A visual with text about the topic.

Demo subject   PHYSICS

         TOPIC   Graphs of motion

Alternative subjects   BIOLOGY   Factors affecting the rate of Photosynthesis

         GEOGRAPHY   Generating electricity by Hydroelectric power (HEP) and bar chart showing countries which generate a significant proportion of their electricity from HEP.

         BUSINESS STUDIES   Organisation chart for a company with notes concerning the job responsibilities.

Preparation

1   Make four copies of the original visual and text.

2   Make a copy of the visual only and removing some key information from the diagram, chart or graph.

3   Write two or three questions about the text and diagram, chart or graph at the bottom of the gapped copy. Copy these sheets, one for each student.

Procedure

1   Put the students into pairs, one A and one B in each pair. Give one gapped copy to each pair. The students both write their names on the copy.

2   Explain that you will display completed copies at the front of the class. Pin these up so that the copies are not facing the students.

3   Tell the students that student A from each pair will walk to the completed copy and find one piece of information they need to write on their gapped copy. They read, hold the information in their heads and return to their partner. They tell the information to their partner, who then writes it on the gapped copy. Check that there is enough clear space for the students to walk safely to and from the displayed copies.

4   Now student B walks and relays the information in the same way. They continue until the gaps are completed and the questions answered. Remove the completed copies and collect in the students' gapped copies.

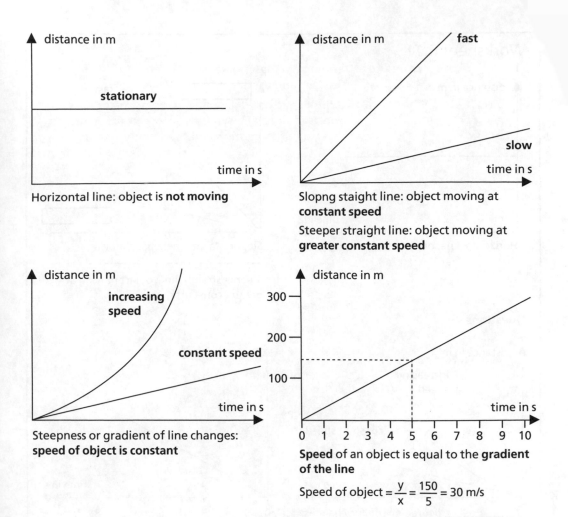

Horizontal line: object is **not moving**

Slopng staight line: object moving at **constant speed**

Steeper straight line: object moving at **greater constant speed**

Steepness or gradient of line changes: **speed of object is constant**

Speed of an object is equal to the **gradient of the line**

Speed of object $= \dfrac{y}{x} = \dfrac{150}{5} = 30$ m/s

5 Give out the second set of gapped copies, one copy to each pair. The students work together to fill in the information. Meanwhile you check that the copies handed in are correct. Give the named gapped copies back. The students check their work.

Variation

Choose a topic and use two or three different visuals about that topic. This stops the students seeing and overhearing what other students are doing. At the end of the activity the students can use the visuals in an information exchange activity.

Worksheet 6.11

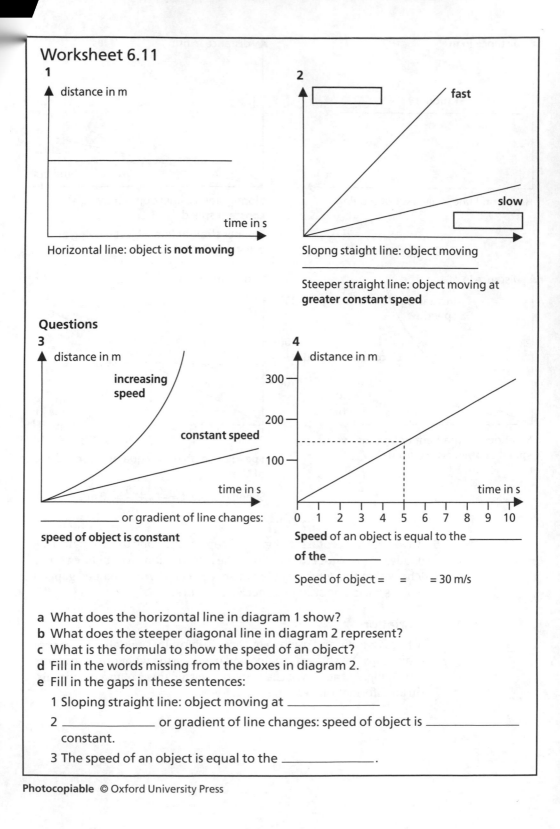

1

distance in m

time in s

Horizontal line: object is **not moving**

2

fast

slow

Slopng staight line: object moving

Steeper straight line: object moving at **greater constant speed**

Questions

3

distance in m

increasing speed

constant speed

time in s

_____ or gradient of line changes:

speed of object is constant

4

distance in m

300

200

100

0 1 2 3 4 5 6 7 8 9 10

time in s

Speed of an object is equal to the _____

of the _____

Speed of object =   =   = 30 m/s

a What does the horizontal line in diagram 1 show?
b What does the steeper diagonal line in diagram 2 represent?
c What is the formula to show the speed of an object?
d Fill in the words missing from the boxes in diagram 2.
e Fill in the gaps in these sentences:

   1 Sloping straight line: object moving at _____

   2 _____ or gradient of line changes: speed of object is _____
   constant.

   3 The speed of an object is equal to the _____.

7

Project work

Projects, whether they are done by individuals or groups, are an important part of course work and examinations. A project should be student-centred and produce a useful and informative end product. How the students arrive at the end product is the 'learning process', and the skills they learn on the way will help them perform in the real world situation. Projects help develop confidence and independence. They are excellent training for the real-life situation in the workplace. Project work also gives the opportunity for students of mixed ability to show their different talents and creativity.

The methodology projects use is varied. They offer group-work experience in researching and collating information. They also encourage the students to research and experience a wide range of materials and resources. In addition, projects teach the students to compare and contrast information and to question and respond to ideas and opinions. Project work is a tool towards student autonomy as they learn to rely more on themselves rather than using you, the teacher, as the main bank of information.

In order to get the full benefits from project work, it needs to be set up, run, monitored, and assessed methodically. The students need to see their efforts being continuously guided, appreciated, and respected. It is better to take one small step at a time towards an extended project. You can then extend and expand the size of the project as you and your students gain in experience and confidence.

This chapter aims to provide guidance on how to set up and run a project, rather than to give examples of numerous subject projects as these will depend on the individual school syllabus. An excellent selection of projects for different subjects, ages, and ability levels can be found in *Project Work* by Diana L. Fried-Booth, in this series.

In this chapter we suggest a complete school project as an ideal opportunity to include the following skills areas required for CLIL:

1 Visuals
2 Listening
3 Guided reading
4 Semi-scripted speaking
5 Supported writing
6 Language awareness
7 Vocabulary/Memory

8   Task design
9   Assessment
10   Networks/Resources
(Source: Keith Kelly)

This chapter will help you prepare and run a school project. The end product will give an overview of how English can be used across the curriculum throughout the whole school. We point out that although students work individually or in small groups during the project lessons, it is important that they still have the security of whole class identity, with each class contributing to a whole school activity. It is also vital that the students see you monitor and assess them individually as well as within the group. If you are asking the students to give real commitment to the project they must, in turn, see that you are doing the same. Projects offer a great opportunity to extend teacher–student and student–student relationships. Assessment and evaluation should be seen to move with ease and respect from teacher to student, from student to student, and from student to teacher.

We have chosen Personal, Social and Health Education (PSHE) as our Demo subject as it includes so many other subjects. However, any subject can be adapted and used to make individual and class projects. The progress and report sheets are simple to follow and can be adapted to suit your own needs.

7.1 Our environment and community

Example of a school project

Aims Speaking and writing skills; note-taking; editing; presentation practice; recording results; developing confidence and independence; using technical equipment and visuals; researching and collating information; time management; assessment and feedback; cooperative learning.

Materials List of areas for study and which subjects to include; digital cameras if available; movie camera if available; Internet access and downloading facilities; lesson progress sheets—one for each group; one copy on OHT to show as an example in lesson one, or one copy to pin up in the class; assessment and feedback sheets—copies as for lesson progress sheets.

Demo subject PSHE (Personal, Social and Health Education—this may come under different subjects in your context)

Topic Our environment and community

Preparation

To prepare for a complete school project requires a meeting of all the different subject teachers who will be involved to discuss, plan, and keep their own notes on steps 1 and 2.

When this is complete and the teachers agree on what is to be included, each subject teacher prepares their own progress report, their personal report sheet, and their assessment and feedback sheets, using Worksheets 7.1a and 7.1b as a guide.

1 List the areas covered in the project.

Example A Preparing to play an active role as citizens
B Developing a healthy, safe lifestyle
C Developing good relationships and respecting the differences between people
D Developing confidence and responsibility and making the most of our own abilities.

2 Write a list of the subjects and what you would like to see included within the subject areas. Decide which class is to tackle which areas.

Example

Mathematics	Financial tools and services; budgeting, saving and managing personal finance.
Religious Studies	Different religions and beliefs in the community; places of worship.
Geography	Physical, human and environmental geography of the area.
Physics	Energy and its distribution and use in the area.
Physical Education	Facilities and opportunities; local sportspeople; training schemes; keeping fit.
Food Technology	Nutrition and diets; local specialities; production and distribution.
Business Studies	Types of commerce and industry in the area.
History	How the past influences the local community.
ICT	The best ways to present the information collected.

3 Prepare a progress report sheet as in Worksheet 7.1a (see page 144) and photocopy one for each student for each lesson or week, depending on the length of the project.

4 Make your own personal report sheets covering group and individual student progress and assessment. Add comments about the group dynamics and time management. Discuss and compare these report sheets regularly with the other teachers involved in the school project.

5 Write and photocopy an assessment and feedback sheet, one copy for each group.

Example

Worksheet 7.1a

Group name _____

Members' names _____

Student's name _____

Subject _____

Subject focus _____

Date _____

Tasks _____

Student's Report
Their progress in the lesson: for example, what was achieved,
what was left unfinished and why, what the student learnt.
This could be factual information or experience.

_____

_____

_____

_____

Tutor's comments _____

_____

_____

Assessment and feedback

_____

_____

- Tutor to Student _____

_____

_____

- Student to Tutor _____

_____

_____

- Student to Student _____

_____

_____

Worksheet 7.1b

Group Name _____

Subject focus _____

Student names _____

_____

_____

Assessment of group research _____

_____

_____

Assessment of the group dynamics
and time management skills

_____

_____

Group presentation skills _____

Assessment grade _____

Feedback from tutor _____

Student feedback _____

_____

_____

Pre-project – planning, organising, task objectives etc.

_____

_____

_____

During project _____

End-of-project assessment_____

Worksheet 7.1c

Topics	Subjects	Sources
Preparing to play an active role as citizens	*Geography— population* *History* *Business studies— professions* *Physics* *Statistics*	*Library reference section* *Internet* *Local Chamber of Commerce* *Textbooks, newspapers etc.*
Developing a healthy, safer lifestyle	*Physical education* *Business studies* *Food technology* *ICT*	*Local authority literature* *Health and safety regulations in industry* *Internet*
Developing good relationships and respecting the differences between people	*Religious studies* *History* *ICT*	*Interviewing local people* *Text books/Internet* *Local newspapers and archives*
Developing confidence and responsibility and making the most of our own abilities	*Mathematics— finance* *ICT* *Music* *Art* *Sport*	*Financial services available locally* *Internet* *Local facilities for the Arts* *Club reports*

Photocopiable © Oxford University Press

Procedure

Lesson 1

1 Introduce the idea of a school project and explain how all the students will be involved. The project could have the name of the area/town/city/district. It could, alternatively, have a title such as 'How and where we live', or 'Our environment and community'. Tell the students that when you research a project you look at it in many different ways, using a variety of academic subjects. That is why all the subjects you are taught at school are equally important in your adult life.

2 Divide the board into three columns and four rows (see the example in Worksheet 7.1c). Write the four subject areas on the board in the first column (these are shown in bold type). Leave room to add comments in the other two columns.

3 Discuss each area with the students. Dictate the following questions: *How do we do that? Where do we find the information? What subjects are we using? How do we present what we find?*

4   Give out a photocopy, one for every student, of the Worksheet but with the second two columns blank. Alternatively, they could copy it on to a sheet of paper.

5   Give the students time to work in pairs to fill in the blank columns. Discuss their ideas as a class and write notes on the board for the students to add to their own copies. Subjects will overlap.

6   Explain to the students which particular subject area their class has been asked to research as part of the overall school project. Put them into groups of four and give them time to discuss and write down possible research areas for their subject.

7   Ask for volunteers to tell the class their ideas. The students listen and make notes.

8   Explain to the students what skills they will be assessed on, when they will be assessed and how they will be assessed. Show them a copy of your assessment and feedback form. Emphasize that assessment will be continual and that they will have the opportunity to discuss it and give feedback to you during all the stages of the project. Emphasize also that working on a project is a good opportunity for them to experience real working-life situations. Explain how important it is to work as a team member and how the appraisal system works in the real working world. All this information could be given in the mother tongue.

9   Give the students time to discuss their project area in their groups. They set individual tasks for the group members.

10 For homework, all students write what they are going to do. This should be presented in note form as their own 'Personal Action Plan', which can be drafted in the mother tongue and then translated with your help into English. This is a useful language activity. You must check these 'Personal Action Plans' before the next lesson.

Follow-up lessons

1   Begin each lesson with the whole class working together. It is useful to ask each group to say one thing about their progress, or give one piece of information they have discovered. It is also good use of class time to check language required and monitor language errors. This focuses the whole class on the project and helps motivation. The students could use this opening period to report on problems they have encountered and discuss possible solutions. Only spend a short time on this lead-in activity. Let the groups begin working as quickly as possible. It is very important that the students learn to manage their time.

2   Monitor the groups carefully. Time yourself carefully when working with them. It is important that you give each group a similar level of attention. In each lesson check and write comments on their 'Progress Report Sheets'.

3 Train the students to work to time. They should allow themselves the final five minutes of the lesson for group discussion. They need to think about what they have done and what has to be done in the following lesson. An action plan is important.

Final lessons

1 Display the project in the main corridors or halls of the school where all the students can see and appreciate it. Visitors to the school can also enjoy the project. The finished project could be used as part of a parents evening.

Each group presents their contribution to the total project. This could be done using a variety of forms.

- One group could use a PowerPoint presentation, another could display picture boards around the rooms or in the main corridors of the school. They could use digital cameras, Internet visuals, video segments, graphs, charts, historical photographs, and so on. Individual written texts would be required to go with the visuals.
- A group could video their own presentation; this video could then be sent to another school or college in the area or in a different country. Lots of schools work together in this way, using English as the lingua franca.
- The school could produce a guidebook on their community. This could be kept as part of a history project. Maybe the local library would display this guidebook.

2 Hold a discussion, feedback, and assessment session.

Comments

1 In a project such as the one in this example, three or four lessons will be enough to concentrate on one particular part of the topic. Students should see their work as an important part of the whole school project. If you allow the project to go on too long the interest level in the overall project drops and the students become too deeply involved in their own subject. This changes the emphasis from a PSHE project back into a subject lesson.

2 During the project the mother tongue will be used from time to time. This gives the students the opportunity to translate and build a bank of new English vocabulary, and to practise and consolidate grammar. It also helps the language teachers to pinpoint problem areas the students need to focus on. The project work from each group should be written and presented in English. Each group must include a vocabulary and reference sheet to be photocopied and given to other class members.

Appendix 1

Language to help you in the classroom

Preparing to start the lesson

Settle down quickly please, let's get started.
Let's just recap on what we did last lesson.
What were the main things we worked on last lesson?

Giving out material

Take one copy and pass them round. Does everyone have a copy?
Pass any spare copies to the front. Thanks.
Share these copies, one between two.

Asking questions

What do you know about…?
Where did you find out about…?
Can you tell me something about…?
How does this work?
Have you ever…?
Do you know where…?
What do you mean by …?
Why do you think this happened?
Why didn't this happen?
What made this work?
What was the reason for this?

Giving instructions

Take a piece of paper. Watch me. Fold it in half and fold it in half again.
Don't start until I give the signal.
Each team must appoint: a time-keeper; an answerer; a messenger; a walker; a speaker; a recorder.
I need two volunteers.
Number yourselves from one to four.
Mix up your slips of paper and share them out.
Take it in turns to…
Sit facing your partner.

Swap papers with your partner (exchange).
Don't let your partner see your picture.
Don't forget to write a note about the information your partner gives you.
Don't panic.
Work alone.
Leave a line after each answer.
You are going to have to remember your partner's information so listen very carefully.
Read silently.
Read out loud.
Everyone in the group must make a copy of…
Jumble the letters of the words. That means mix them up.
Decide if the statement is true or false.
If you need me come and get me.
Put up your hand.

Identifying and numbering

Write the numbers 1–10 down the side of a page.
Choose one of the words from the list to put in the gap.
Match the words to the pictures.
In the first box … next to the box write … under the box write … draw a quick diagram of … in the last box.
Re-order the sentences
Underline the key words in the passage— only the key words.
Don't forget which letter/number you are.
Give me an example of…

Write your words all over the board—not in a vertical list.
Write the words in random order.

ook at the word that is underlined/in
   italics/in bold.

Scoring and marking

You get a point for every correct answer.
You only get a point if your word is exactly
   the same as the one on the sheet.
Don't forget to keep your own score.
   Add up your score.
Put a tick if it is right, and a cross if it
   is wrong.

Grouping and moving students

Go and sit in the groups you were in
   last lesson.
Find a new partner to work with.
All the A students get together, all the
   B students get together.
Walk round the class and ask as many
   students as you can about … in the time.
Mix and mingle. That means talk to as
   many other students as you can during
   the time.
Don't spend too long talking to the same
   person. Keep moving.
Everybody stand up and make a circle.
Make two circles of ten.
Now you are in a circle. Turn so you
   are facing the back of the person in
   front of you.
Turn and face your partner.
Turn to the right/left.

Analyzing

To try this out…
To prove this…
Follow the steps in the experiment
   to show how…
If you look at it this way, you'll see…
Think about the ways of testing…
Read it carefully and pick out the points
   that show/relate to/indicate…

Checking

Is that clear?
Any questions before we start?
Talk to the person next to you and tell each
   other what you have to do.

What's the problem?
Call out the name of another student. That
   student must try to answer the question.
If you don't know the answer, pass the
   question on to someone else.
Check your answers with the rest of
   your group.
See if your partner agrees with you.
Compare your answers with the person
   next to you.

Encouraging and redirecting

Comments to use when helping students individually

That's good so far. Now try to…
What you have written here is clear and
   interesting. Well done.
That's the right idea.
Keep to the point.
You need to go into more detail here.
What do you mean by this exactly?
Explain this to me, as if you were the
   teacher. Good. Now write it like that.
Check your facts here.
Have you thought about…?
Maybe you should say more about…
I don't quite follow your point here.
You have put a lot of work and effort in
   with this. Good.
You would get good marks for this.
You don't seem to have any problems.
   Good.

Timing

Remember to time yourselves
You only have a few minutes left.
Keep an eye on the time.
I'm only giving you five minutes to do this.

Ending the lesson

Let's go over what we have learnt today.
Check that you've copied everything from
   the board.
Finish this off for homework.
You've worked well today. Good.

Appendix 2

Useful language for your students

Asking for and giving opinions

Do you think we should...?
How do you feel about...?
What do you think about...?
I think...
I think it would be a good idea to...
As I see it, we should...
On the other hand...

Asking each other questions

What do you know about...?
Where did you find out about...?
Can you tell me something about...?
How does this work?
Have you ever...?
Do you know where...?
What do you mean by...?
Can you give me the name of a...?
What does ... mean?
What is ... called?

Cause

Because of climate changes the deserts
  are expanding.
Due to climate changes the deserts
  are expanding.
Owing to climate changes the deserts are
  expanding.
Because the climate is changing the deserts
  are expanding.
As the climate is changing the deserts
  are expanding.

Result/effect

The climate is changing, so the deserts
  are expanding.
The climate is changing, therefore the
  deserts are expanding.

The climate is changing, consequently the
  deserts are expanding.
The climate is changing, as a result the
  deserts are expanding.

Classifying

These are all types of data storage.
This is a variety of vertebrate animal.
You can divide these into three categories.
It's made up of two different elements.
It can be divided into five sections.
Welding involves melting and fusing
  metal together.
The whole plant can be broken down into
  three main parts.
The different elements of Alkali
  metals are...
The orchestra is split into/divided into
  different sections.
Deciduous woodland ecosystems consist of
  trees that shed their leaves in winter.

Comparing and contrasting

The colours used in this painting are
  stronger than those used by other artists
  of the period.
Plastic is more flexible than many other
  materials.
Some of the most useful information about
  this subject can be found on the website
  I've given you.
The largest rise in population was in the
  late 1940s.
It is as important to study the agriculture
  for this area as it is to study the industry.
Her foreign policy was not as successful as
  her domestic policy.
The results are identical.

...mpared to/with other political leaders of the time, he was more democratic in his approach.

His style of writing is similar to Ernest Hemingway's.

This generation's approach to the problem was different from that of previous generations.

The match we expected in the results didn't happen.

People's opinions about this vary.

Pixel-based software is not the same as vector-based software.

Conclusions

The end result is…

It follows that … would happen.

My conclusions are…

This makes me think that…

This means that…

Defining and describing

It's a sort of/kind of measuring device.

It's something like a piano but it produces a totally different sound.

It's something we use to measure temperature.

It's something used for measuring temperature.

It looks like a barometer.

It's similar to the invention we talked about earlier.

You'd find this when looking at paintings of the same period.

You would see this in a castle, for example.

It's made of animal skins.

It's made up of different kinds of animal skins.

It's used for measuring temperature.

It's a device for heating chemical substances.

It's a system for describing climate change.

It's an instrument for cleaning bottles

Evaluating

The importance of this is…

This is useful to…

This is important because…

Interpreting visuals

This picture/graph/diagram/chart shows us that…

If you look at this chart you will understand why…

The diagram illustrates this.

Predicting and hypothesizing

If we do this, then … will happen.

To get the result we should…

Unless we do … we will not be able to…

This could happen because…

One result could be…

If we do it this way, we should see…

Sequencing

First of all, secondly, then, following this, next, the next step/stage is to, after that, finally

Spatial

…in the box at the top of the page…

…in the top right-hand corner…

…at the bottom of the picture…

…at the end of the passage/text…

…underneath this…

…directly below…

…in the centre of…

…to the right of…

…in the next column…

…by the side of that…

…parallel to…

…outside/inside the box…

Appendix 3

Useful books

General background to CLIL

Grenfell, M. (ed.). 2002. *Modern Languages Across the Curriculum*. Abingdon, Oxfordshire: Routledge Falmer.

This book describes research and case studies throughout Europe, recent trends and issues, and how CLIL is developing across Europe. It also offers practical materials and useful ideas for teachers and policy-makers.

Kroschewski, A., A. Schuenemann, and **D. Wolff,** 1998. *A Resource Base for Bilingual Educators*. Jyväskylä, Finland: University of Jyväskylä. ISBN 9-513-90282-X.

A multilingual bibliography of research and teaching materials for CLIL.

Masih, J. (ed.). 1999. *Learning Through a Foreign Language*. Stirling: Scottish CILT. ISBN: 1902031687.

A collection of papers giving European perspectives on the way to structure CLIL.

Jacomelli, P. (ed.). 2001. *ETAS Journal* Volume 19, No. 1. (English Teachers' Association Switzerland. To order a copy, email admin@e-tas.ch.)

This journal contains a special supplement entirely devoted to CLIL with contributions from a number of CLIL experts, including reports on the pilot CLIL project in Zurich.

Subject-based materials

Bell, P. 2000. *The Primary School Curriculum 2000 Topic Book*. Broughton, Preston, UK: Topical Resources. ISBN 1-872977-55-3; email: sales@topical-resources.co.uk

Although this book is written for primary level it could be useful for the lower secondary grades in CLIL. It covers programmes of study in Science, Technology, History and Geography, and is fun to use.

Birdsall, M. 2001. *Cross-Curricular English Activities*. Leamington Spa: Scholastic.

An extensive collection of photocopiable ready-made activities in English for maths, geography, life skills, history and science.

Littlejohn, A. and **D. Hicks.** 1997. *Cambridge English for Schools*. CUP.

This is a coursebook for learning English across the curriculum which adopts a communicative task-based approach with regular revision and evaluation.

Revision guides

BBC GCSE Bitesize series

Coordination Group Publications GCSE Revision series

Letts GCSE revision series

These three series each consist of a series of revision guides for a wide variety of different subjects. They contain clearly presented visual information and sample exam questions.

Multiple intelligences

Campbell, D. 2003. *Teaching through Multiple Intelligences*. Boston, Massachusetts: Allyn and Bacon.

An excellent survey of multiple intelligences. Full of valuable classroom activities, resources, materials for assessment, and ideas for interdisciplinary units.

Puchta, H. and **M. Rinvolucri.** 2005. *Multiple Intelligences in EFL*. Innsbruck: Helbling Languages.

This is a concise overview of the latest research into human intelligence with practical suggestions for the teaching of adolescent and adult students. It contains 74 clear and easy-to-follow classroom activities.

Other

Deller, S. and **M. Rinvolucri.** 2002. *Using the Mother Tongue*. Addlestone, Surrey: Delta.
This book offers ideas on the judicious use of the mother tongue to improve the efficiency, speed and enjoyment of learning another language.

Fried-Booth, D. 2002. *Project Work*. Second edition. Oxford: Oxford University Press.
This provides a wide variety of immediately accessible ideas for projects inside and outside the classroom. Activities can be used with a wide range of levels and age groups. They need a minimum of preparation and each activity is explained in full – with aims, resources, preparation and implementation, and feedback.

Gardner, B., and **F. Gardner.** 2000. *Classroom English*. Oxford: Oxford University Press.
This is an accessible guide to using English in the classroom for non-native speaker teachers. The book is in two parts: Section 1 provides advice on issues such as how to check that learners have understood, and when to use English. Section 2 looks at different situations in the classroom, for example, 'Using the coursebook' and 'Giving instructions'.

Hughes, G. S., J. Moate, and **T. Raatikainen.** 2007. *English for Classroom Management*. Oxford: Oxford University Press.
This practical handbook is for trainee teachers who want to acquire accurate, authentic, and idiomatic classroom language, and for experienced teachers who want to extend the range of their classroom English.

Hedge, T. 2005. *Writing*. Second edition. Oxford: Oxford University Press.
This book presents a range of techniques for encouraging good pre-writing and drafting strategies. It helps learners to develop paragraphs coherently, to use cohesive devices, to use a range of sentence structures, and to develop appropriate vocabulary.
The activities involve students in reviewing their work, revising it, and editing the final draft.

Hillyard, S and **R. Sampedro.** 2004. *Global Issues*. Oxford: Oxford University Press.
This book focuses on real-world issues to encourage communication skills, reflection, and critical thinking.

Lewis, G. 2004. *The Internet and Young Learners*. Oxford: Oxford University Press.
Organized according to topic area, and within each area by web search, communication, and web creation activities.

Rinvolucri, M. 2002. *Humanising Your Coursebook*. Addlestone, Surrey: Delta.
This provides a wide range of original imaginative humanistic activities and techniques to give new life to any coursebook.

Salaberri, S. 1986. *Classroom Language*. Oxford: Macmillan.
Sections include 'Simple Instructions', 'Dealing with the language of spontaneous situations', 'The language of social interaction', 'Pair and Group work', 'Question types', 'Using audio-visual aids', 'Dealing with errors', and 'Evaluation'. Each section starts with a questionnaire and ends with a progress chart.

Svecova, H. 2003. *Cross-Curricular Activities*. Oxford: Oxford University Press.
A selection of thirty units covering a wide variety of cross-curricular topics aimed at upper-primary and secondary classes. Areas covered include mathematics, geography, biology, history, music, art, and drama. All the activities give learners opportunities to communicate in English and at the same time explore core areas of the curriculum.

Windeatt, S., D Hardisty, and **D. Eastment.** 2000. *The Internet*. Oxford: Oxford University Press.
This gives detailed examples of classroom activities that exploit the opportunities offered by the web, including searching on the web, evaluating web pages, creating language learning material, and communicating using the Internet.

Appendix 4

Useful Websites

Any subject

www.oup.com/elt/teacher/rbt
www.howstuffworks.com
www.letts-education.com
www.biography.com
www.bbc.co.uk/schools/teachers
www.bbc.co.uk/schools/gcsebitesize
www.onestopenglish.com
www.euroclic.net
www.factworld.info
www.thinkquest.org/library
www.teachersnetwork.org
www.homeworkelephant.co.uk
www.teacher.scholastic.com
www.education.leeds.ac.uk
www.armoredpenguin.com
www.scholastic.com
www.enchantedlearning.com
www.iearn.org/
www.abcteach.com
www.webquest.sdsu.edu
www.primaryresources.co.uk

Art

www.impressionism.org/
www.poster-und-kunstdrucke.de/images

Business Studies

www.businessweek.com
http://news.bbc.co.uk

Design and Technology

www.design-technology.org

Food Technology

www.foodtech.org.uk/
www.projectgcse.co.uk/food/

Geography

http://library.thinkquest.org/11922/habitats.htm
www.discovery.com/exp/exp.html
www.nationalgeographic.com/resources/ngo/education/

History

www.historyworld.net
www.historytoday.com
www.bbc.co.uk/history/historic-figures
www.SchoolHistory.co.uk

Literature

www.bibliomania.com

Mathematics

www.mathgoodies.com
www.cut-the-knot.com
www.allmath.com
www.mathworld.wolfram.com

Music

www.reggaefusion.com
www.essentialsofmusic.com/composer

Personal, Health and Social Education

www.europarl.eu.int

Physical Education and Sports Science

www.netfit.co.uk

Religious Studies

www.omsakthi.org/religions

Sciences

www.planet-science.com
www.phschool.com/science/planetdiary/archive

http://whyfiles.org/
www.scienceacross.org
www.bbc.co.uk/science/space/
www.spartechsoftware.com/reeko/
www.schoolscience.co.uk

www.wastewatch.com
The companion website to this book and
series, www.oup.com/elt/teacher/rbt
provides regular updates to the
information and ideas in this book.

Index

present perfect tense 6.5
presentation 1.6, 6.10, 7.1
project work 10, 133–40, 7.1
pronunciation 1.11, 1.14, 3.1, 4.1
  of the alphabet 3.4, 4.1, 4.2
purposes/uses, stating 6.9, 6.11
questionnaire use 3.3
questions
  asking and answering 1.7, 2.6,
    3.3, 3.5, 4.11, 5.5, 5.12, 5.13, 6.2,
    6.4, 6.5, 6.6, 6.7
  asking *wh-* 1.1, 6.9
  forms 16, 143, 1.1, 2.2, 3.5,
    5.12, 6.1, 6.4
  giving short answers 5.11
  responding quickly to
    written 4.11
  understanding 5.11
  writing 3.7, 4.11, 5.11, 6.1
  writing *what is/what are* 5.10
  yes/no 1.1
reading 10, 17, 133, 1.7, 1.9, 1.13,
  1.14, 1.15, 4.7
  aloud to correct the teacher
    1.10
  and listening 6.11
  and repeating statements 1.11
recording 5.6, 7.1
reference books 145–6, 6.10
repetition 17, 1.11, 1.12, 4.2
reporting back 1.5
research 113–32, 134, 6.6, 6.10,
  7.1
  and follow-up 6.6, 6.7
  sources for 6.3, 6.5
resources
  using fellow-students as 3.2
  using supplementary 10,
    113–32, 145–8, 4.8, 6.4, 6.5,
    6.7, 6.10
revision 10, 93–112, 2.4, 3.2, 3.4,
  3.7, 4.9, 4.11, 5.9, 5.13, 6.3
  of key points 5.14
  of key words 3.5, 6.2, 6.9, 6.11
  lists 3.6
  oral 3.1, 3.3
scanning (skimming) 16, 1.5,
  1.6, 4.7, 6.11
sentences
  beginnings to complete 4.6
  correcting 5.1
  expanding 4.5
  re-ordering 1.13, 5.2
  recognizing 1.15

sequence, memorizing a 1.8,
  1.10
sequencing a text 144, 1.10, 3.1
signs 4.9, 6.9, 6.11
spatial language 144, 1.9, 6.2
speaking 10, 59–73, 133, 1.14,
  3.3, 3.4, 3.6, 3.7, 7.1
spelling 75, 1.13, 2.5, 4.1, 4.2, 4.6,
  5.2, 5.9
student-generated activities
  45, 2.5, 2.6, 4.11, 5.5, 5.6, 6.4
summarizing 75, 4.5, 4.7, 4.8, 4.9
superlatives 6.10
symbols 4.9, 6.9, 6.11
talks, giving short 3.6, 3.7
technical equipment, using
  113, 7.1
technical terms 1.3, 2.6
textbook language,
  understanding 1.3
thinking
  in depth 3.1
  and writing at speed 5.14
time management 7.1
translating 1.5, 1.15, 2.6, 2.8, 5.1, 5
video 6.8
visualizing 2.4, 2.5
visuals
  interpreting 144, 6.1
  using 113, 133, 6.1, 6.2, 6.3, 6.4,
    6.8, 6.11, 7.1
vocabulary 10, 45–58
  building 45, 1.16, 2.7
  expanding and consolidating
    topic 5.9
  learning 4.10, 6.9, 6.11
  recalling 133, 2.3
  revising specific 2.1, 2.2, 5.2,
    5.3, 6.9, 6.11
word associations 2.1
word order 1.7, 5.2
words
  categorizing 2.1, 2.7
  definitions of 4.9, 6.2
  focusing on key 17, 1.2, 1.3
  guessing 5.4
  labelling on a picture 2.5
  listening for key 1.2, 6.8
  matching descriptions to key
    5.2, 5.8
  memorizing key 2.4, 2.6, 3.6
  re-ordering 2.5
  recognizing and
    understanding key 5.3

revision of key 3.5, 6.2
  understanding key 5.3, 5.8
writing 10, 59, 75–91, 133, 1.2,
  1.12, 1.14, 4.6, 4.7, 7.1
  comments and questions 6.1
  editing 4.4, 4.6
  formal academic style 1.3
  mixed language functions in
    4.3
  questions and definitions
    5.10
  and spelling from listening
    1.13
  and thinking at speed 5.14
  true/false statements 5.6

Subjects taught

Art 1.1, 1.12, 1.14, 1.16, 2.5, 2.8,
  5.11, 6.3
Biology 1.9, 1.12, 2.1, 2.2, 2.5, 2.6,
  2.8, 3.2, 3.3, 3.4, 3.6, 3.7, 4.1, 4.5,
  4.11, 5.1, 5.2, 5.5, 5.6, 5.7, 5.9, 5.13,
  6.2, 6.3, 6.11
Business Studies 1.3, 1.5, 2.1, 2.2,
  2.3, 2.7, 3.5, 4.5, 4.8, 4.9, 4.10, 5.1,
  5.2, 5.7, 5.8, 5.12, 5.14, 6.2, 6.5, 6.9,
  6.11
Chemistry 1.10, 3.4, 4.2, 4.3, 5.2,
  5.4, 5.8, 5.10, 5.12, 6.7, 6.10
Design and Technology 1.1, 1.2,
  1.3, 1.6, 1.7, 1.10, 2.3, 2.4, 2.5, 3.1,
  3.2, 4.1, 4.8, 4.10, 4.11, 5.13
Environmental Studies 2.4, 4.2,
  4.8
Food Technology 1.1, 1.2, 1.6,
  1.10, 1.13, 1.14, 5.6, 5.14, 6.2, 6.6,
  6.9, 6.10
Geography 1.3, 1.12, 1.16, 2.2, 2.7,
  3.1, 3.2, 3.3, 4.2, 4.3, 4.5, 5.1,
  5.3, 5.4, 5.7, 5.9, 5.12, 5.14, 6.1, 6.3,
  6.4, 6.7, 6.8, 6.9, 6.10, 6.11
History 1.2, 1.8, 1.9, 1.10, 1.11,
  1.12, 1.13, 1.16, 2.1, 2.6, 3.3, 3.4,
  3.5, 3.6, 3.7, 4.3, 4.6, 4.8, 4.10, 5.3,
  5.5, 5.6, 5.11, 5.13, 5.14, 6.4, 6.5
ICT 1.11, 2.4, 2.8, 3.1, 4.3, 4.9, 4.10,
  4.11, 5.2, 5.9, 6.4, 6.6
Literature 1.5, 1.8, 1.11, 2.3, 3.1,
  3.4, 3.7, 4.6, 5.3, 5.10, 6.6, 6.10
Mathematics 1.1, 1.8, 1.9, 1.11,
  1.14, 2.5, 2.6, 2.8, 3.5, 3.7, 4.1, 4.11,
  5.1, 5.3, 5.7, 5.8, 5.10, 5.11, 6.3, 6.6
Music 1.7, 1.9, 2.3, 3.6, 4.1, 4.2, 4.5,
  4.9, 5.4, 5.5, 5.9, 5.10, 5.12, 6.5